Praise for *Receiving From Your Angels*

"As an angel ambassador, Jill Kempner brings forth the love of the angels in her debut book, *Receiving From Your Angels.* Throughout its pages, her gentle and authentic guidance takes you on a path of self-compassion and healing, transforming your pain into peace. This book is a must-read for those that are ready to open to the compassion of the angelic realm."

– **Sunny Dawn Johnston,** Psychic Medium and Author of the bestselling book, *Invoking the Archangels*

"*Receiving From Your Angels* is a must-read for earth Angels seeking to embody the benevolence of the Divine. Working alongside the Angelic Realm for over 11 years, with the intention and focus on helping you heal pain, author and Angel Professional Jill Kempner guides you to take excellent care of your physical, Spiritual and energy body. This beautiful book is a gift to the reader, filled with authentic Angel awareness providing much-needed healing."

– **Dr. Marni Hill Foderaro**, Survivor, Speaker and Author of the award-winning Spiritual fiction *God Came To My Garage Sale*

"Very excited that Jill has written a book based on Angel Healing using her own life experiences and the techniques she has perfected to live a pain free life. As a former client I know the powerful work she does through her Angel Wisdom and healing. This book couldn't be coming out at a better time. Jill shares four easy to use practices that help you understand how to work with your Angels to become pain free. This book will benefit so many."

– **Debbie N Silver,** Transformational Coach
and #1 International Bestselling Author

"Jill has woven wisdom from the angels with her personal stories of growth and challenge, sharing powerful tools for living a joyful, pain free and angelic supported life. Jill's pure and loving spirit shines through in the inspiring angel guidance she shares in *Receiving From Your Angels.* This book absolutely supports how many ways one can have a positive and healthy approach to life by choosing to welcome the support of the angels."

– **Dee Crowley,** LCSW

"As an angel professional, Jill Kempner walks her talk. She shares from a place of authenticity and real-life experience, which makes her a powerful and loving teacher of angelic wisdom. Her genuine, loving relationship with the angels is inspiring and an important reminder of the beautiful, healing relationship we're all meant to have with these loving beings."

– **Lisa Espinosa,** Spiritual Career Coach and
Award-Winning Author of *Answering Your Inner Calling*

"Jill's book gives you the feeling that we are not in this journey alone, and we are surrounded by angelic help constantly. It's an easy read and leaves you with a very comfortable and uplifting feeling."

– **Eric Soderholm,** founder of
SoderWorld Healing Arts Center

RECEIVING FROM YOUR *Angels*

Four Practices to Heal Your Pain with Angel Love

JILL KEMPNER

INSPIREBYTES OMNI MEDIA

Receiving From Your Angels:
Four Practices to Heal Your Pain with Angel Love

This book is intended as a reference resource only, and does not purport to give medical advice. The instructions and methods presented herein are in no way intended to be a substitute for medical or psychological treatment from licensed health-care professionals. The author of this book does not dispense medical advice nor prescribe the use of any technique as a form of treatment for physical or medical problems without the advice of a licensed medical professional, either directly or indirectly. The intent of the author is only to offer information of a general nature. In the event the reader uses any of the information in this book for themself or others, they are assuming full responsibility for their choices and actions. The author and the publisher assume no responsibility or liability for the actions of any reader.

Distributed globally with Expanded Distribution by KDP.
ISBN Paperback: 978-1-953445-16-2
ISBN E-Book: 978-1-953445-17-9
Library of Congress Control Number: 2021949271

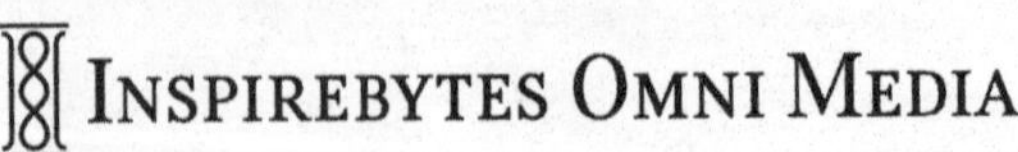

Inspirebytes Omni Media LLC
PO Box 988
Wilmette, IL 60091
For more information, please visit www.inspirebytes.com.

This book is dedicated to those courageous earth angels who came here to transform pain into peace. You are safe to spread your wings, embody the benevolence of the Divine, and share your unique light with the world. I see you!

Dear Lauren, earth angel extraordinaire

Thanks for all you do! ♡

Be a master of self-love! ♡

Keep shining.

all my love.

Jill Kempner

Table of Contents

Introduction

Welcome, earth angels, and those seeking natural pain relief. I'm thrilled your angels led you to this book. If you are experiencing pain right now, the angels and I are sending you armfuls of love. I pray this book brings you the healing and pain relief you need.

This book is designed to offer angelic pain relief. I hope to help you open channels to receive love from your angels to heal your physical pain. Your pain relief is my mission.

This book contains four practices that walk you step-by-step through relieving pain by receiving love from your angels. In each practice, I share a personal story to support your learning. My personal experience led me to create these steps and practices to angelic pain relief. I know firsthand that these pain-relieving practices work because the experiences I went through were how these practices were created.

I write this book virtually pain-free today because of these healing practices. I have also helped many clients and students become pain-free angel receivers too!

Although I feel this book can help anyone in pain, I wrote it for earth angels. I want to share some of the characteristics of an earth angel to provide a framework for who this book can best serve.

Earth angels are highly sensitive and highly intuitive. You can sense your loved ones' emotions and feel them in your body and heart. You can sense or even know what others are thinking. You can hear the whispers of your angels, even if you deny or dismiss them at times. You can even sometimes "see," either visually or in your mind's eye, auras, colors, and flashes of angel light. You can sense energy beyond normal human limits with ease.

As a sensitive soul, you treasure your body-soul connection. You respect your body as the sacred home of your soul. You may have food sensitivities or strong reactions to certain foods, beverages, and substances. Your body reacts instantly to fear or love, and you trust your body's truthful wisdom. You know your physical body and your energy body well, and you are devoted to taking care of both daily. As an earth angel, you know that your physical body, the temple of your soul, is meant to carry the benevolence of the Divine.

Deep within you, there is a strong sense—or knowing—that you have been here before. You know in your heart that you have lived many lives and are devoted in this life to being a channel of unconditional love. Some earth angels have experienced childhood challenges like trauma, abuse, or pain that eventually opened you to the spiritual realm. You have a strong connection with the unseen realms, like fairies, dragons, unicorns, and, of course, angels. You know you have a mission here on earth, even if you don't know all the details.

Amongst their many gifts, earth angels are resilient. You courageously bounce back as you face your pain, wounded parts, and issues with gentleness and compassion. You know there is a gem at the center of the boulder of pain. You have the ability to discover the lesson and blessing within the deepest pain you have experienced. This devotion to unconditional love transforms your pain into peace.

Earth angels are both bold and humble. You boldly know you are magnificent because so is everyone. You humbly understand that we are all equal and that when one person heals, we all heal. You know it is important to shine your light—not because you are better than anyone, but because when you shine, we all shine.

Of course, you can increase your shine by relaxing your body and mind, releasing pain, and receiving love from your angels everyday. Conscious relaxation is a gift you give yourself that clears your energy, calms your mind, and keeps your heart open to your angels' infinite love and compassion.

Medicine heals. I see each practice in this book as medicine. Angelic pain relief medicine. You can expect your pain to diminish and disappear, your heart to open wider in self-compassion, and your connection to your angels to strengthen from working the medicine of these practices. The medicine of your angels is only potent if you give yourself permission to receive it. The more willing you are to receive love from your angels, the more love they have to give to you. Remember, the love of the angels and archangels is unlimited because they are fueled by Source love.

The angels will solve your pain relief issues with grace, compassion, and unconditional love. Your deepest wound is your greatest treasure. The angels say that when fear is ready to release, it shows up as pain. Your angels know the source of your pain and how to relieve it. All you have to do is ask and receive.

The fuel of this book, meaning the energy woven into the words in these pages, is peace, ease, compassion, unconditional love, and pain relief. This means that even holding this book in your hands has a healing effect. Of course, total pain relief will come from working the medicine of each practice with a willing heart.

Your angels want you to be pain-free so you can channel more of their love and light to the earth. Physical or emotional pain slows the flow of your angels' love. Through your devotion to receiving the angels' love, you will receive lessons and blessings from your pain.

Your soul is in a constant state of receiving love from your angels and the Divine. It's pain that blocks you from receiving and trusting the steady flow of love. It's not like sometimes the angels are sending you love, and sometimes they're not sending you love. Your angels are always sending you streams of unconditional love. Your goal is to become aware of this angelic love and give yourself permission to receive it.

My desire is that you know and feel your angels' love for you. My hope is that this book helps you feel confident and safe receiving love from your angels to heal any pain. I want you to have the tools that honor your body as the home of your soul. Each angel practice is a healing tool that is filled with the medicine of divine compassion and unconditional love. My intention is that you always have access to angel love, which provides pain relief, spiritual growth, and both individual and collective ascension.

Your angels have the remedy for all that ails you, and they have deep compassion for your healing journey. Receiving your angels' medicine for your specific pain, whether physical or emotional, is why I am writing this book.

I think learning how to receive love from your angels matters because as earth angels, you are here to bring peace to the earth. You are here to enact and embody God's will of peace on earth. God does not want you to suffer, be in pain, or struggle. God sent you angels and archangels to assist your journey. Saying yes to your angels is saying thank you to God and the benevolent universe.

Your pain has a purpose. Your pain is the doorway to the angel medicine that heals it. Your healing is directly connected to your personal ascension and the evolution of the planet. Transforming your pain into peace uplifts the earth and humanity. Your personal pain relief matters to God, the angels, and Mother Earth.

Why Receive From Your Angels?

It is important to understand why you are choosing to receive from your angels. Your crystal-clear intention will create a strong angelic connection, and this connection will help heal your body.

Receiving means to take in, accept, experience, or welcome. So receiving means to welcome and accept the love and healing of your angels, which heals any pain, whether that pain is physical or emotional. Below, the angels share a few reasons why you would want to receive love from your angels.

Reason #1: To reclaim your magnificence

As an earth angel, you are here to experience your divinity and allow yourself to be a channel for unconditional love. The truth is that everyone is called to be a channel of unconditional love. Reclaiming your magnificence is answering the call and aligning your will with divine will to channel unconditional love.

Reclaiming your divine magnificence heals you and the world. Your angels say that your main mission here on earth is to learn to love all of you, the Light and the Shadow. You are here to embody the love and benevolence of the Divine.

Earth angels are humble and know that reclaiming your magnificence is not about being better than anyone else. You lovingly reclaim your magnificence because we are equal, and everyone is magnificent. When you claim your magnificence, you allow others to do the same. As an earth angel, you are guided to see yourself through the eyes of your guardian angels. You are encouraged to love yourself the way your guardian angels love you.

As you learn to love your whole self, you raise your personal vibration and the vibration of the planet. Your angels never ever judge, shame, or berate you. They hold you with great respect and reverence. Your angels honor your wisdom and your courage to embody so you can share your earth angel gifts. Your angels see past any seeming errors you might believe about yourself. They see the magnificent light in your soul and guide you to do the same.

Reason #2: Experience peace, wholeness, and connection

Part of reclaiming your magnificence is remembering that your soul is whole. Your soul can never be damaged or broken. Your soul is vast and filled with peace, compassion, and unconditional love. The pain you have experienced is actually your ego or your parts inside that have forgotten your divinity. When you allow yourself to receive love from the angels, your angels connect your soul to your body. Your body-soul connection brings deep peace and relief to any pain you're experiencing. This relief brings wholeness and allows more of your earth angel medicine to be shared.

Reason #3: Self-knowledge

The Greek aphorism "know thyself" provides a framework of self-discovery that allows you to share more of your earth angel gifts with humanity. When you know and love yourself, this provides a secure foundation that allows you to be of service with great compassion and understanding. When serving others, you can only take someone as far as you have taken yourself, which speaks to the message of "know thyself," or as the angels say, "love thyself."

Your angels know and love every aspect of you. Your angels know your lessons, your earth angel gifts, and your pain. They also know the shadowy aspects of yourself that you hide or would rather ignore. The angels help you know and love yourself better by encouraging the divine qualities of self-love, self-acceptance, and self-compassion.

The gateway to self-knowledge is self-love. When you allow yourself to receive love and messages from the angels, it's actually about knowing and truly loving your whole amazing self! Your angels know that when you love yourself, this invites others to love themselves. All this self-love raises the vibration of the planet.

Reason #4: Heal pain

Remember that your pain has a purpose. Your pain is actually a portal for angel love to enter. The pain—or issues in the tissues—that you are experiencing today is part of your soul's lessons and part of your earth angel medicine. Every pain or issue has a deeper meaning and spiritual understanding that you came here to discover and heal.

The pain you feel is not a punishment. The pain is a soul-chosen lesson for you to understand and transform. Your body agreed to carry your soul's light, and your soul agreed to be contained in your body. Your guardian angels agreed to guard and protect all of you. When your body experiences pain, it's asking for more love.

Receiving love from your angels is a gift you give to yourself. Inviting the angels to heal your pain, whether it's physical or emotional pain, is a way of expressing gratitude for the gift of the angels and your life. You are meant to be happy and pain-free, and your angels stand ready to ensure this reality comes true.

How To Use This Book

The book has been divided into three parts to support your physical body to heal, your heart and mind to sync, and your soul to soar on your angels' wings.

Part I: Angels 101 begins with an introduction to the angels, including your guardian angels and the archangels, so you can become familiar with their energy and presence.

Part II: Your Energy Body 101 outlines the four layers of your energy body—roots, parts, chakras, and aura—that allow you to increase your ability to receive love from your angels. This part of the book holds a special place in my heart because I am simply fascinated with the sacred relationship between the physical body and the energy body.

The third part encompasses the four distinct practices I developed to connect with your angels to heal physical pain. Each practice has its own section and begins with a personal story linked to that practice. Thereafter, each practice contains:

- A teaching
- The steps to the practice combined with an explanation of the practice
- The archangels of the practice
- A guided angel meditation to close the practice

These practices were created to help you receive more love from your angels. Each of the practices focuses on a specific aspect of connecting with your angels. They are:

- Practice One: Renew Your Devotion — Devote yourself to healing your pain.
- Practice Two: Relax and Cherish Your Body — Relaxation is the gateway to angelic pain relief.
- Practice Three: Release and Lead with Your Heart — Let go and let your loving heart lead.
- Practice Four: Receive and Trust Your Intuition — Allow and trust intuitive guidance.

As you work the medicine of each practice in this book to heal your pain, your body, heart, mind, and your intuitive channels will continue to open to your angels' messages and love.

PART ONE

ANGELS 101

Chapter One

Who Are Your Angels?

An angel is defined as a divine being who acts as an attendant, agent, or messenger of God. The angels are limitless beings of love and light who can move through time and space with ease. The angels have no egos, no bodies, and no gender. However, the angels will often appear gendered to be more relatable. Many times, angels appear in human form with wings.

I see God as the essence of pure, unconditional love. In this book, I will use many names to describe this essence of pure, unconditional love, like: God, Source, Great Spirit, the Creator, the Divine. I invite you to use the term for the pure essence of unconditional love that most resonates with you at this time.

I often get asked the question, "Why would I connect with the angels when I can connect directly with God?" I love the way my teacher, Kyle Gray, answers this question, which I have paraphrased here:

> *Imagine God as a huge heart. Every time God's heart beats, an angel is created. You can also imagine God as a huge brain or mind. Every time God thinks a thought, an angel is created. Therefore, the angels are the heartbeats and thoughts of God. When you ask the angels for help, guidance, and pain relief, you are communicating directly with God.*

God is thrilled when you work with the angelic realm because, to the Divine, there is no separation. God, the angels, and your soul are one. When you experience pain or fear, you have stepped into separation and forgotten your divine oneness with the Creator. God and the angels will never judge, shame, or berate you when you feel pain. They will send a healing wave of love and compassion.

Angels are messengers of the Divine, bringing you messages directly from your soul and Source. Your angels' messages will always be loving, positive, trustworthy, peaceful, and constructive. An angelic message will never, ever cause you or anyone else harm. The angels have the same code as physicians and healers: "Do no harm." The angels have no agendas; they are only here to serve unconditional love. Angels are an extension of God's unconditional love.

Your angels are like your best friends. They love, know, and honor all of you, and you can tell them anything. Your angels love you for who you are right now; you don't need to change in order to receive their love. Of course, your angels will help you heal and evolve as you invite them to assist you.

One fascinating thing about the angels is that they are multidimensional beings. This means that your angels can be in multiple places at the same time. This is a difficult concept for our human minds to accept. Your angels are right here and right now in this present moment, but they can also go forward and bless your future and go back and bless your past. Your angels live outside of linear time in the quantum field, and they can transcend time and space with ease. Your angels have access to divine solutions and miracles that your humanness cannot yet embrace.

Your angels are bridges of light that lift your humanness up so you can connect with Source energy. Your angels love you unconditionally and are always with you. *Your angels are always sending you love.* It's not like sometimes the angels are sending you love, and sometimes they're not sending you love. The angels are always sending you streams of love and light. Although the angels' love remains constant, that love can be harder to sense when you experience fear or pain.

Your perception of the angels' love can waver when you experience issues in the tissues like stress, tension, anger, pain, fear, unresolved grief, negativity, and trauma. More precisely, you are not really asking your angels to send you love. Instead, you are asking that you *become aware* of this love—that you open your perception and begin to *receive your angels' steady flow of love.*

Every single person has angels. It is your birthright to be fully supported by the Divine, which includes direct access to all of your angels' love and support. Whether you are atheist or don't believe in angels, you still have angels.

There are three levels of awakening to your angels:

1. Acceptance — Accepting you have angels, even if you can't see or hear them yet.
2. Willingness — Being willing to receive their love, support, and healing energy.
3. Receiving — Consciously receiving your angels' love and support.

On the path of the earth angel, you are stepping forward and devoting to consciously and purposefully receiving from your angels.

Your angels never force their love upon you, and although they are forever with you, because of your free will you must *ask* them to increase your awareness of the love they are already sending.

About the Law of Free Will

The key to opening the flow of conscious, pain-relieving support from your angels is to simply *ask!* Asking invites your angels' infinite flow of support, help, and guidance. Asking is essential because Source created you with the gift of free will. Free will is a way to ensure that you do not feel controlled by the Creator. You need to ask for help with each and every situation, issue, event, and pain. Your free will is not to punish you, it is to give you the spiritual freedom to grow at your own pace.

God gave you the gift of freedom to make your own choices and decisions. The gift of free will allows you to make autonomous choices that support your highest path of spiritual growth and independence. God never judges your decisions. The Creator sends you signs, synchronicities, and 100,000 angels to support your highest path of growth and healing.

The gift of free will can sometimes be misunderstood, as some may feel that God has abandoned, rejected, or exiled you. This is far from the truth, as God knows you are never truly separate from your loving Creator. Whenever you begin to feel this pain of separation, God sends even more angels to your side to remind you how loved you always are.

How Your Angels Communicate With You

Your angels communicate with you directly through your heart. Your heart is the gateway to your angels' love. Your angels' unwavering mission is for you to receive a steady flow of unconditional love, which nourishes your body like fresh blood feeds the muscle of your heart.

Angels communicate with you through your:

- Heart
- Body and energy body
- Thoughts and mind
- Feeling and emotions
- Intuitive channels

Angels also communicate with you through:

- Signs
- Synchronicity
- Music
- Numbers
- Oracle cards
- Other people

Your angels' messages are always peaceful, positive, and trustworthy. Your angels will never cause you or anyone else harm. When you receive angelic messages, it will feel like a sigh of relief, like a weight has been lifted off you. Time and time again, my clients say they feel so much lighter or light as a feather. That's angelic pain relief.

Your angels, who are always with you sending you love, communicate with you in many ways. They send you thoughts in your mind to assist you. Your angels send you images and visions to guide you. Your angels share messages through your feelings and your body to support you. They send you smells to awaken your senses and bring you into the present moment. Your angels send you messages through other people, music, numbers, signs, synchronicity, and oracle cards to awaken your consciousness to their unending love and support.

Chapter Two

Guardian Angels

When your soul was created, you were assigned two guardian angels to be with you for eternity. Your guardian angels:

- Have been with you since birth.
- Know the details of your soul's mission.
- Guard and protect you.
- Love you unconditionally.

Your guardian angels live outside of time in the quantum field and can move through time and space with ease. Even though your guardian angels are right here and now sending you love, they can also bless and heal your past and your future. No matter how much pain you are in, your guardian angels have access to all the knowledge, support, and healing you need to restore health and wellbeing.

Your guardian angels have been with you since the creation of your soul. Before you were born into this life, your soul had a divine meeting with God and all of your angels and guides, including your guardian angels. You chose your family, your birthdate, and astrological sign as well as your challenges and issues. Therefore, your guardian angels know every detail of your divine life mission.

Your guardian angels know your full potential as well as the way through each and every pain, fear, or challenge you will ever face. They even know your chosen exit points from the earth when you go back to Spirit. This is not a morbid thought because returning to Spirit is a joyous occasion even though it can seem very sad from a human perspective.

Your guardian angels are just that: guardians. They are here to protect you from harm or an untimely death. Your loving Creator would not send you here without support and protection. Remember, you have to ask your angels for help with each and every situation.

There is an exception to that rule: If you are going to be injured or die before your time, your guardians can and will intervene for your highest good. I will always remember when my guardian angels protected me from a car accident when I was pregnant with my second child.

> *I was about 5 or 6 months pregnant, and I was pulling up to a red light near my home. I was going to make a right-hand turn. I had stopped at the red light and looked to see if it was clear to go. I was about to take my foot off the brake and accelerate into the turn when I felt a presence on my shoulder and heard, "Look again."*
>
> *By the grace of God, I paused. I looked again, and a car raced past. I would have been side-swiped if I didn't pause to look again.*
>
> *This was when I was first getting introduced to the angels. Before I knew anything about what I am writing in this book, I knew to thank them. I felt so grateful to be spared that potential injury and to the angels for protecting me and my baby from harm.*

That event was a wake up call for me to pay more attention to my angels. I felt a newfound safety with the angels that has only continued to grow. Even though I had not expressly asked for help, my guardian angels knew that the accident was not part of the bigger plan, and they were able to intervene and help. *Thank goodness I listened.*

Your guardian angels' main purpose is to love you unconditionally. You can increase your ability to receive more love from your guardian angels by thanking them for their help, eternal love, and protection. The gratitude you send to your guardian angels is actually more for you, though. Your guardian angels know that when you thank them, your heart opens. When your heart opens, you are more receptive to their love.

Your guardian angels are made from pure Source love. All angels come directly from the heart and mind of your Creator. As you've already read, every time God thinks a thought, an angel is created. Every time God's heart beats, an angel is created. So angels—including your guardian angels—are the thoughts and heartbeats of God.

As I mentioned, many people question why you would work with the angels instead of directly with God. The main reason is when you experience pain, you have forgotten your divine connection. When you are in pain, stressed, worried, anxious, or experiencing a trauma, your vibration is lower, and this can make it difficult for you to connect directly with God. *The angels work as bridges of light that connect your humanity to your divinity.*

Your guardian angels meet you where you are with respect and great compassion, and they instantly raise your vibration so you can receive Source love once again. All you have to do is ask for their help. Your guardian angels never judge your pain and will restore your personal peace when you invite them to help you. *Your guardian angels' love is unceasing and will guide you away from pain and toward peace.*

Chapter Three

Archangels

Archangels are limitless beings of love and light who can be with each person simultaneously. Additionally, the archangels:

- Have no egos, bodies, or agenda other than to serve you.
- Have no fear of your shadow.
- Raise your vibration.
- Offer unconditional love and support.
- Connect you with your own unlimited potential.

As unlimited, non-denominational beings of love, you never have to worry that you are taking the archangels from bigger or more important tasks. It is only your humanness that limits the infinite power of the Divine. The Divine is omnipresent, meaning everywhere at once. Remember: Angels, including the archangels, are the thoughts and heartbeats of God and can be with each person simultaneously. The nature of unconditional love is that the more pure love you receive, the more it expands. There is an infinite amount of love for each and every soul on the earth.

The archangels vibrate at a higher frequency than your guardian angels. Archangels are like the managers of your guardian angels and provide unlimited protection, support, and divine guidance to keep you connected to your soul's mission. Each archangel is an infinite being of love and light, and as an extension of God's love and benevolence, they stand ready to heal your pain. Each archangel has a specific medicine that can help your body heal.

Archangels, like all angels, have no egos, no bodies, and no agenda. The archangels have no gender; however, they use gender to be more relatable to humanity. The archangels are beyond any one religion, but they come through and are woven into all major religions. This is a divine synchronicity.

The archangels are messengers of God, who deliver divine messages that heal your shadow. The very fabric of their being is created from pure, unconditional love. The archangels are not afraid of your shadow. They will never judge, shame, or shy away from your pain, but will instead ceaselessly shine their heart light into every dark crevice of your body, mind, and heart.

In each practice, I discuss inviting the archangels. Inviting the archangels into your daily life makes the Creator's heart so happy. The archangels are gifts from God that are intended to be utilized by humanity. When you receive love and healing from the archangels, you are expressing deep gratitude and appreciation to God. The gratitude you express allows you to be a greater channel of Source love for your body and the earth.

You will meet four archangels for each practice who will support you in deepening your connection to the practice. Here are five steps for invoking the archangels:

1. Ask for their help by using the Archangel Invitation.
2. Relax your body and mind.
3. Release resistance, pain, tension, and blocks to receiving.
4. Receive the archangels' healing energy and medicine.
5. Say thank you.

The mighty archangels are only here to serve unconditional love and to enact God's will of peace on earth. As an earth angel, it is your sovereign right to ask for the archangels' abundant help and support. When you accept the archangels' help in healing your pain, you are thanking God and the loving universe.

PART TWO

Your Energy Body 101

Chapter Four

Your Energy Body

Your energy body is a gift from God designed to keep you connected to the Divine and your amazing angels. Like your angels, your energy body is part of the non-physical world, and you need to use your inner vision and imagination to connect with it. As a sensitive soul and earth angel, it's important to cultivate the sacred relationship between your physical body and your energy body.

Earth angels are here to embody the benevolence of the Divine. One way to embody the benevolence of the Divine and experience angelic pain relief is to take excellent care of both your physical body and energetic body in equal measure. You want to approach your whole energy body with respect, gratitude, and a humble heart.

What does embody mean? Embody means to be an expression of, or to bring a feeling or energy into a tangible form.

Embodying the Divine means:

- You are inviting the unconditional love of your angels in your physical body/energy body.
- You are allowing that love to fill your cells, heart, and chakras.
- You are receiving angel love in your physical being and not just in your mind.

Earth angels are invited to walk with a conscious awareness of your energy body to stay in the flow of your angels' love. Your angels are pure energy. It is easier for your human body to receive the angels' healing energy—which creates pain relief—by working with your energy body.

Four Layers of Your Energy Body

There are four layers of your energy body that support angelic pain relief highlighted in this book. Understanding your energy body will increase your capacity to receive loving pain relief from your angels. These four layers of your energy body include:

- Energetic roots
- Universe of parts
- Chakras
- Aura

Your energy body is designed to:

- Protect your physical body
- Release pain from your physical body
- Receive angelic love
- Support your body-soul connection
- Keep you connected to your angels

Protect Your Physical Body. Your energy body offers an invisible layer of protection both within and around your physical body. The strength of your energy body is only as strong and potent as the attention you give it. Remember: Energy follows intention. As you bring your conscious awareness to your energy body, you strengthen its protective ability alongside your angelic connection. If you are completely unaware of your energy body, it's likely to become cluttered, diminishing its ability to serve and protect you.

Release Pain From Your Physical Body. Your amazing energy body can clear and release pain from your physical body. Each layer of your energy body is intrinsically connected to a physical body elimination system. This connection allows pain and other non-serving energies to be released from your physical body. Each of these physical elimination systems expels toxins from your body that don't serve you. The layers of your energy body and their physical elimination systems, include:

- Energetic roots—colon or bowels (digestive system)
- Universe of parts—liver, kidneys, and lymphatic system
- Chakras—lungs (respiratory system)
- Aura—skin (integumentary system)

Receive Angelic Love. Your energy body actually receives love from your angels first, before your physical body. As part of the non-physical world, your energy body is just that—pure energy. Your angels are also pure energy, so it is easier for your human body to receive love from your angels through your energy body first. This allows for a smoother transfer of energy, ultimately making it easier for your human body to receive your angels' love. This smoother energy transfer and connection is not for the angels, but for you. The energy body acts as a receiver, like an antenna receiving radio waves that allows the pure, loving energy of the angels to flow into your physical body, relieving pain.

Support Your Body-Soul Connection. Your physical body is designed to carry your soul's light and embody your angels' love. Your physical body is the vehicle through which your soul chose to grow and evolve. Your energy body is made up of your earth angel medicine, your soul's light, and the unconditional love of Source. Each of these elements creates a magnetism that supports your body-soul connection. When you heal pain from your physical body, more of your soul's light can be grounded into your body and onto the earth.

Keep You Connected To Your Angels. Your awesome energy body vibrates at a higher frequency than your physical body. This higher frequency attunes to your angels' love, which keeps you connected to your angels. Your angels are always sending you love into your energy field, increasing your ability to receive their love and healing. When you experience pain, your energy body opens to receive your angels' love. Your angels can send you loving pain relief through your energy body, which deepens your connection to your angels. As you receive angelic pain relief through your energy body, you strengthen your divine connection.

Let's explore your awesome energy body!

Chapter Five

Energetic Roots: 1st Layer of Your Energy Body

Your roots are the energetic equivalent of the roots of a tree. Your energetic roots are the foundation of your energy body and serve to connect your body to the earth. Although you may not be able to see your roots with the naked eye, you can use your imagination to access them. Your roots move with you everywhere you go, providing instant grounding that gets you out of your head and into your body.

Building a relationship with your roots creates a stable foundation for your physical body and consciousness to be present in each moment. Your angels are always guiding you into the present moment because this is where your angels are, right here and right now.

Your roots are connected to your root chakra at the base of your pelvis. They flow down your legs, similar to the blood that flows through your blood vessels. Your root chakra is connected to your hips, pelvis, sacrum bone, perineum, legs, knees, and feet.

Your energetic roots are designed to:

- Ground
- Release
- Receive
- Connect you to Mother Earth

Grounding. The densest part of your physical body is your bones. Your skeletal system protects your organs so they can function. Your bones give structure for your muscles to move. Your energetic roots are support for your physical body, like bones are for your organs. Your roots support your physical body in staying grounded to the earth.

When you are grounded, you are more receptive. Receptivity is the key to angelic pain relief. When you are in pain, there may be a desire to numb or escape from your body. Your angels have so much compassion for this tendency and encourage you to stay present and grounded. Being rooted and grounded will heal the pain faster than numbing or escaping.

Some earth angels struggle with feeling or staying grounded because the density of the earth plane feels heavy or burdensome at times. There is a desire to float heavenward to feel light again; however, your mission on earth necessitates you staying grounded. Grounding helps you listen to your body, be present in the moment, and be more receptive to your angels' love. Grounding also anchors your soul's light both into your physical body and into the earth, blessing you and the earth.

Releasing. Your roots have the ability to eliminate pain, toxins, and unhelpful energies out of your body, similar to your intestines releasing waste material after digestion. Releasing what no longer serves you is an ongoing process and happens in layers. You cannot release what you are not ready to release. Releasing can be so subtle that you don't feel anything. Other times, releasing may feel intense, and your body may twitch, shudder, or move involuntarily. Releasing can also cause the rise and fall of your emotions. Try not to resist the releasing process; instead, focus on your breath and relaxing your body and mind.

Consciously sinking your roots into the earth to release negative or unhelpful energy is a daily practice. When sending roots of light into the earth, it's essential to focus on gratitude for Mother Earth. This is important to note: You are not poisoning or damaging Mother Earth by releasing toxins into her soil, crystals, or tree roots through your energetic roots. Mother Earth is the greatest healer, as she has the ability to take any negative energy and transform it into usable energy once again. Mother Earth's loving and generous energy transforms all that you release, no matter how toxic, into compost and fertile soil, instantly and properly. Just remember to express your gratitude and say thank you.

Receiving. Your roots can also receive the love, compassion, and nourishment you need from the earth, your soul, and the angels. Your roots receive healing energy and love similar to how your intestines receive and assimilate the nutrients from the food you eat. Like your intestines absorb the vitamins and nutrients your body needs to thrive, your roots can receive the love, healing, and compassion you need to heal any pain.

Receiving means to assimilate or take in through your senses. Receiving through your roots may feel like taking a deep breath in, or it may feel like you're being nurtured or cared for. In the beginning, you may not feel or notice much while you receive through your roots, and that's totally normal. Just keep practicing; your roots' awareness and sensitivity will grow with time and attention.

Connecting to (and Blessing) Mother Earth. Consciously sinking your roots into the earth is a loving way to give back to Mother Earth for her love, support, and abundance. Allowing Mother Earth to receive *your* soul's light and earth angel medicine blesses you and her. This reciprocity with Pachamama strengthens your ability to release more and receive more. As an earth angel, you are meant to bring and create heaven on earth. You are meant to be an open vessel for Source love to flow through you, for your own healing, and for the earth's healing too.

Ways to Access Your Roots

There are many ways to access your energetic roots. In my experience, the five most common and effective ways include:

- Meditation
- Intention
- Visualization
- Physical relaxation
- Root and earth star chakra

The deeper your roots go into the earth, the more you can open your upper chakras and receive from the higher angelic realms. This grounded connection creates space in your body anchored in higher vibrations of love and compassion to clear pain or any issue in the tissue. Your energetic roots can connect through:

- Groups (your soul cluster family or another group of people)
- Crystal medicine
- Trees and plant medicine
- Ancestors

Connecting Roots With Groups. When you connect your roots with others in a group, you do this in an interdependent way with healthy boundaries, not co-dependently. There is no fixing, rescuing, or absorbing others' energies or pain when you connect your roots with a group. When you connect your roots, you will not absorb what anyone releases, nor will they absorb anything from you.

Connecting roots with others amplifies and strengthens your ability to release more and receive more. It's important at the end of a gathering to disengage your roots from the group while still staying connected to the earth.

Connecting Roots With Crystal Medicine. Crystals are Mothers Earth's gems and a gift from her to humanity. Crystals, like your angels, have a great purpose of serving unconditional love. When you consciously connect with them, you are helping the crystal fulfill its purpose. Crystals, like your chakras, are angel receivers and have the ability to anchor in divine light and love. Crystals can help you stay grounded, transmute energy, support healing, and increase your ability to receive love from your angels. This is why many earth angels are drawn toward working closely with the crystal kingdom.

When you consciously sink your energetic roots into the earth, you can send your roots as deep and wide as they want to go. It's important to trust the wisdom of your roots to connect with the crystal medicine that can most serve you. You do not need to consciously know all about a crystal to receive its healing properties. Through your intention, your body can receive the medicine of the crystal energetically. The crystal medicine then brings healing and pain relief.

Connecting Roots With Trees and Plant Medicine. The wisdom of the trees is profound. Trees are the ancient ones, and they have much medicine to share. Tree medicine can provide support, unconditional love, and a safe haven. Connecting your roots to tree roots or plants is another energetic support that blesses you and the earth. Your body can release pain and receive peace from this tree root connection. The natural pain relief you can experience while connecting your roots to the wisdom and love of the trees and plants displays the generosity of the earth.

Connecting Roots With Ancestors. When you choose to connect with your ancestors, you want to connect with their wisdom, love, and miracles, not the trauma or the drama. Set your intention to connect with those holy or elevated ancestors who love you unconditionally to ensure a connection of the highest integrity.

Your ancestral root connection allows you to integrate your past life gifts into the present moment. Creating a root connection with your beloved ancestors allows you to receive the blessings, medicine, and love of your ancestors. You can also send healing to your ancestors through your roots to release unhelpful karmic patterns from your cellular DNA. Roots through the right leg connect with the paternal side of your family, and the roots through your left leg connect to the maternal side of your family.

Disengaging Roots. When you are leaving a circle or closing a meditation, you set your intention and visualize your roots being drawn back to yourself, lightly disengaging from the group. Inhale and draw your roots back toward your own energy body. Exhale as you re-ground into the heart of Mother Earth. This is done to seal the meditation and to shift from the energy of the collective back to just your own independent energy. As sensitive souls and earth angels, this is a reminder to not carry anyone else's pain or burdens.

Chapter Six

Your Universe of Parts: 2nd Layer of Your Energy Body

The next layer of your energy body that is essential to understand on the path of the earth angel is your inner universe of parts. Parts work is a psychotherapy model created by Dr. Richard Schwartz, also called Internal Family Systems, or IFS.

Internal Family Systems are easily likened to a symphony orchestra, with your soul as the intended leader and your parts playing music in harmony to support your soul.

- Your soul is the conductor of the orchestra.
- Your parts are the musicians playing musical instruments.
- Your parts want your soul to lead, but they become imbalanced when they forget this connection and dynamic.

Your parts are your humanity, and your angels love *all* of your parts. Your parts are an aspect of your energy body that allows you to express your unique gifts and talents. They offer room for growth and evolution. It's only when parts become imbalanced that pain arises. Some key points to know about your parts:

- Parts are real, not imaginary, and they live in non-physical reality, just like your angels.
- Parts live in your body and have issues in the tissues. Your soul is whole.

- Parts have noble intentions; they are protecting you even if it appears they are sabotaging you.
- You cannot get rid of your parts; however, they can transform, evolve, and rebalance.
- You have three main categories of parts: managers, firefighters, and exiles.
- You have happy, balanced, and joyful parts.
- Parts are accessed through emotional relaxation.

The elimination system of your physical body representing your universe of parts includes the vital organs of the liver, kidneys, and lymphatic systems. The liver is a blood-recycling warrior and performs over 500 functions. Your kidneys balance fluids, regulate blood pressure, and filter out waste. Your lymphatic system is connected with your immune system and helps fight off infections. Just like you cannot live without your liver, kidneys, or a functioning lymphatic system, you cannot live without your human ego parts.

Your parts are very real and not simply something made up by your imagination. Your parts are also known as your ego. Although the parts are subpersonalities created by your mind, you always want to approach your parts with deep respect and compassion.

Your parts are like the angels because they live in the non-physical world; they are pure energy, like the angels. Even though you may not be able to "see" the angels or your parts with the naked eye, it does not make them any less real. Some earth angels can "see" their parts with their inner vision and clairvoyance.

Your parts live inside your body. Your mind, which created these subpersonalities, is intimately connected with your physical body. Cherishing your physical body creates space for your parts to be seen and healed by the angels. Angelic pain relief is about healing your body and the parts that live there.

Your soul is whole and is continuously receiving love from the Divine. The pain you are experiencing is a part that is calling out for help. When you have any issue in the tissue, it's actually a part that is experiencing the pain or issue. Accepting that you have a universe of parts living inside your body creates space between you (your soul) and the pained part. Knowing this changes how you perceive and heal the pain.

Your parts are meant to help and support your life. Your parts aspire to be the devoted followers of your soul and are not supposed to lead the way. Your parts gladly follow your soul until they become imbalanced. When a part becomes imbalanced—meaning it is consumed by stress, anxiety, or pain—it can get loud and try to take over your consciousness.

No part of you is "bad." All of your parts have noble intentions, even if it appears they are sabotaging or harming you. In many instances, your parts are simply trying to protect you. Your angels know and love all of you and invite your parts to rebalance.

As energy can never be created nor destroyed, only transformed, you can never get rid of your parts. Actually, it's a part that thinks you can get rid of a part. The only exception to this rule is if you are carrying someone else's part. The angels can help the other person's part to go back to their home with love. As a sensitive and empathic soul, you can unknowingly carry your partner's, children's, or parents' parts.

You—meaning your soul—alongside your loving angels, are simply rebalancing your parts. You can rebalance your parts by:

- Thanking your parts
- Asking the question, "What do you need?"
- Inviting emotional relaxation
- Allowing this pained part to receive love from your angels

There are three main categories of parts: Managers, Firefighters, and Exiles. All of these categories have parts that need to be rebalanced and reconnected with your soul as the leader.

The Managers:

- Are focused on organizing the day-to-day activities that operate your human life.
- Love to check things off the to-do list and feel most accomplished when they are "doing."
- Are meant to be loyal followers of your soul. They often forget this and try to lead the way.
- Are constantly trying to fix, manage, and control situations or issues, and keep the exiles from flooding the system with pain or trauma.

The Firefighters:

- Have sudden, impulsive reactions to an exile's pain.
- Are designed to put out fires when the exiles get triggered.
- Save or rescue you from pain.
- Tend toward excitement, fun, and thrills as a means of escape.
- Numb and distract you from being overwhelmed by the exile's pain.

Firefighters may use unhealthy coping skills to numb or distract you, like abusing drugs and alcohol, overeating, anger, disassociation, thrill-seeking behaviors, and impulsiveness.

The Exiles:

- Are shadow parts of you that hold pain and trauma.
- Can be your wounded inner child.
- Hold great treasures when balanced by your angels.
- Have the issues in the tissues like shame, fear, anger, judgment, harshness, negativity, frustration, and guilt.

- Are the parts that you try to hide, ignore, push away, or deny.

The firefighters and the managers are protectors of the exiles. The firefighters numb and distract, while the managers control and create order to avoid having the exiles flood your system with pain.

Pain as a Part

The angels want to highlight one loud and often exiled part, which is pain. Let's be honest: Pain is not fun. Pain can trigger lots of feelings, such as feeling crabby, exhausted, grumpy, and stressed. Pain is an unpleasant experience that causes you to pause. Pain blocks your joy, creativity, and your light. Pain can feel like a cloak of darkness and heaviness that stops your light from shining. Your angels are on a mission to heal your pain so you can receive long-lasting physical pain relief and shine your light on earth.

What Is Pain?

Pain is defined as an unpleasant sensory and emotional experience associated with actual potential tissue damage. The angels say that when fear is ready to release it shows up as pain.

For our purposes, we define pain as follows:

- Pain is an experience for your soul and has a purpose.
- Pain can strengthen your earth angel medicine.
- Pain offers soul growth and healing.
- Pain is a teacher.
- Pain is a portal for angelic love.

The angels emphasize that as humans, although we may claim to "hate" pain, some can often become very attached—or even addicted to pain and the chemicals it releases in your body.

As a human you can:

- Take the pain personally.
- Judge the pain.
- Worry and stress about the pain.

When you experience physical pain in your body, this is not a punishment. From the angelic perspective, pain is a teacher. Pain can teach you to:

- Shift, learn, and grow.
- Slow down.
- Wake up.
- Be compassionate, gentle, and patient.
- Change direction.

What do the angels say about pain? The angels have taught me that pain is pain. Your angels know that the pain you feel is real. The moment you experience any pain, your angels send you extra waves of compassion and healing to soften and relieve your pain.

You angels will never:

- Compare your pain with others' pain.
- Diminish or minimize your pain.
- Judge your pain.

Your angels will always:

- Invite you to learn the lesson from the pain.
- Support you in transforming the pain.
- Send you cushions of compassion to soften pain.
- Invite you to pause and tend to even the smallest pain.

If you can pause when you have pain and ask the question, "What lesson am I learning from this pain?" you will find the path of ease and release much faster.

Chapter Seven

Chakras: 3rd Layer of Your Energy Body

Chakras are spinning energy centers that move energy. Chakras both transmit and receive energy. These spinning energy centers run along the length of your spine from just below your feet in your earth star chakra to the highest point of your aura well above your crown, the stellar gateway chakra. Your chakras are the access point between the physical body and your aura.

Chakras are:

- Spinning energy centers known as wheels, disks, or vortexes.
- Angel receivers where you give and receive love from your angels.
- Visualized as both flowers or temples with healing chambers for your parts.
- Where your earth angel medicine is stored and accessed.
- Naturally expanding and contracting to clear pain and excess energy.
- Accessed through mental relaxation.
- An interdependent system.
- Designed to receive intuitive messages from your angels.

As humanity evolves, so too does your energy body. The chakra system provides instant feedback from your environment and is always receiving love from your angels. The chakra system has evolved from seven rainbow chakras to 13 spiritual chakras.

Characteristics of the seven physical body chakras:

- Root, sacral, solar plexus, heart, throat, third eye, and crown
- Three dimensional
- Rainbow colors
- Visualized as flowers in 3D
- Linked to seven major nerve plexuses
- Many earth angels are still operating on the 3D level

Characteristics of the 13 spiritual chakras:

- Eight body chakras: root, sacral, navel, solar plexus, heart, throat, third eye, and crown
- Five spiritual chakras: earth star, ear, causal (halo), soul star, and stellar gateway
- Visualized as temples in 5D
- Five dimensional
- Evolved colors, many crystal-clear
- Designed to support your soul in staying connected to your angels while in your human body
- Create space in your physical body and aura for angelic love and soul's light to enter
- Lie dormant or inactive until you consciously open them

You can access your chakras through mental relaxation. Mental relaxation means slowing down your busy, fluctuating mind. Your energy body, including your chakras, is part of the non-physical world, so you need your imagination and your open mind to access your chakras. Mental relaxation calms your mind so you can clearly communicate with your chakra system.

Here is a list of the 13 spiritual chakras and their corresponding role or meaning. Each chakra is further defined with more detail, following this list:

1. Earth star—anchoring soul into body and onto earth
2. Root—grounding and safety
3. Sacral—ease
4. Navel—flow
5. Solar plexus—peace and forgiveness
6. Heart—unconditional love
7. Throat—clear communication
8. Third eye—unconditional trust and inner vision
9. Ear—hearing your angels
10. Crown—illumination and innocence
11. Causal—divine downloads
12. Soul star—soul's mission
13. Stellar gateway—Source connection

The 13 Spiritual Chakras Defined

1. Your **earth star chakra** is located in your aura, approximately 18 inches below your feet, and is supported by Archangel Sandalphon. Your earth star chakra is designed to keep your soul anchored in your body and onto the earth.
2. Your **root chakra** is connected with your hips, back, bowels, and bones, and is supported by Archangel Michael, Archangel Gabriel, and Archangel Ariel. Your root chakra is designed to create safety, stability, and strong foundations.

3. Your **sacral chakra** is connected with your womb, sacrum bone, and reproductive organs, and is supported by Archangel Gabriel. Your sacral chakra is designed to allow ease and support creative expression of your emotions.
4. Your **navel chakra** is connected with your kidneys, bladder, and lower spine, and is supported by Archangel Gabriel. Your navel chakra is designed to invite passion, flow, and harmony.
5. Your **solar plexus chakra** is connected with your liver, gallbladder, pancreas, stomach, spleen, and adrenals, and is supported by Archangel Uriel and Archangel Raziel. Your solar plexus chakra is designed to vibrate peace and forgiveness and align your personal will with divine will.
6. Your **heart chakra** is connected with your physical heart, lungs, and thymus gland, and is supported by Archangel Chamuel and Archangel Ariel. Your heart chakra is designed to radiate unconditional love to all of your parts and chakras. Your heart chakra is an alchemical space.
7. Your **throat chakra** is connected with your throat, esophagus, thyroid, parathyroid glands, mouth, and jaw, and is supported by Archangel Michael and Archangel Gabriel. Your throat chakra is designed to speak your truth with love and courage.
8. Your **third eye chakra** is connected with your physical eyes and master glands, and is supported by Archangel Raphael and Archangel Raziel. Your third eye chakra is designed to help you trust your inner vision and see

the light in yourself and others. Your third eye is the chakra that helps you envision your energy body.

9. Your **ear chakras** are the spiritual chakras connected with your physical ears, inner ear organs, and atlas and axis vertebrae, and are supported by Archangel Michael, Archangel Zadkiel, and Archangel Orion. Your ear chakras are attuned to hear the voice of your angels, your body, and your parts.
10. Your **crown chakra** is connected with your brain, cranium, and nervous system, and is supported by Archangel Uriel and Archangel Jophiel. Your crown chakra is designed to receive innocence, joy, divine thought, miracles, and illumination from your angels.
11. Your **causal chakra** is considered the halo chakra and is located above and behind the crown chakra. Your halo is supported by Archangel Christel. Your causal chakra is designed to confidently receive divine information from your angels. This spiritual chakra, like the others, lies dormant until consciously activated.
12. Your **soul star chakra** is energetically located more than 18 inches above the crown and is physically connected with your shoulders. Your soul star chakra is supported by Archangel Zadkiel, Archangel Amethyst, and Archangel Ariel. Your soul star chakra contains the blueprint of your soul's mission and is designed to bridge your humanity and your divinity. Your soul star chakra contains both your karma (patterns) and your dharma (great purpose).
13. Your **stellar gateway chakra** is the highest point of your aura and is physically connected with the back

of your neck. Your stellar gateway chakra is supported by Archangel Metatron and is your direct connection to Source. All your prayers are heard and answered though your stellar gateway chakra, and this chakra temple stores much of your dormant earth angel medicine. Once this chakra is activated, your ability to receive love from your angels is amplified.

Chapter Eight

Aura: 4th Layer of Your Energy Body

The fourth level of your energy body is your aura. Your aura is designed to be able to receive messages from your environment and provide real-time feedback from your surroundings. Each layer of your energy body is designed to keep you connected to your angels, especially your aura. Tending to and maintaining a clear and balanced aura is one of the jobs of your angels. However, because you have free will, you have to *ask* the angels for help with healing and clearing your aura.

Your aura or energy field is:

- An electromagnetic shield that protects your physical body.
- Visualized as egg-shaped and can be 4–20 feet in diameter around your physical body.
- Varied in size, strength, and adaptability depending on your awareness of its presence.
- One unified field but categorized into four layers.
- Semi-permeable, not a wall or barrier.
- Accessed through spiritual relaxation.
- Connected to the physical elimination system of the skin.

If you are completely unaware of your aura, it will be smaller and not as strong and protective. If you take care of your aura, its protective and supportive abilities will be greatly enhanced. The physical elimination system connected with your aura is your skin. Just like your skin is the largest organ of your body designed to protect your tissues and eliminate toxins, so is your aura designed to protect and empower your physical body.

Four Layers of Your Aura

Each layer of your aura has its own unique function and purpose to protect your body. The four layers of your aura are:

- Physical
- Emotional
- Mental
- Spiritual or karmic

Each layer of your aura vibrates at a different frequency from the most dense and lowest frequency at the physical layer to the least dense and highest frequency at the spiritual layer.

The physical layer of your aura:

- Is closest to your physical body.
- Is vibrationally the densest layer.
- Stores the blueprint of your physical body, including each muscle, bone, and organ system.
- Stores imprints of physical pain, trauma, and disease.

The emotional layer of your aura:

- Touches the physical layer and is less dense.
- Contains your emotional memories and experiences.
- Is the most difficult to map out because it is always in motion.
- Stores every emotional experience you've had—from joys, celebrations, and successes to pain, fear, and trauma.

- Is the rich layer of the aura and needs to be tended to regularly.
- Is magnetic and intimately connected to the mental layer.

The mental layer of your aura:

- Stores thoughts, ideas, and beliefs.
- Touches the emotional layer.
- Vibrates at a higher frequency.
- Makes it challenging for you to access the angels because you have over 70,000 thoughts per day.

The spiritual layer of your aura:

- Vibrates at a high frequency.
- Is where your angels and guides reside.
- Is the container for your karmic patterns that you came here to heal in this lifetime.
- Stores prayers, wishes, and desires.

Your aura is a vast and protective electromagnetic field that may store many energies. Knowing what energies are in your aura empowers you to take charge of your own energy and pain relief journey. As my teacher, Kyle Gray, says, "You are the keeper of your mind and body." When you practice being a good steward of your aura, you can release the pain of regret, blame, and victimhood that slows the flow of your angels' love.

Now, let's look at what is in your aura, as well as further defining each aspect.

What's in Your Aura

- Imprints
- Leaks
- Holes and tears

- Psychic attack weapons
- Non-serving energetic cords
- Your amazing earth angel medicine

Imprints:

- Are impressions of all of your physical issues, emotions, thoughts and karmic lessons.
- Can be empowering and positive or restrictive and painful.
- Are aspects of your active or dormant earth angel medicine.
- Remain until you learn the lesson.

Leaks:

- Are restrictive karmic patterns that are currently active in your life.
- Are activated places where you give your power away.
- Create poor boundaries.
- Are caused by saying yes when you want to say no.

Holes and tears:

- Are like bruises or cuts on your skin.
- Consist of weak or vulnerable places in your aura that can allow your energy to leak out.
- Are the places you allow negative or dissonant energy to enter.
- Are common for earth angels.

Some of the common causes of leaks, holes, and tears include: suppressed emotions (anger, fear, sadness, etc.); trauma; alcohol and drugs; exhaustion or lack of sleep; chronic pain or physical injury; environmental toxins; and unintentional psychic attacks from people (negative thoughts, criticism, betrayal).

Psychic attack weapons:

- Are daggers, knives, swords, hooks, and chains.

- Are often the source of mysterious or "out of the blue" pain.
- Are common and nothing to be ashamed of or worried about.
- Can be both intentional or unintentional and can even be carried over from past lives.

Non-serving energetic cords:

- Formed when worry, blame, or fear enters a relationship, both consciously and unconsciously. Everyone has cords.
- Can resemble surgical tubing and can work in two directions.
- Can attach to not only people, but also places, situations, objects, and even memories.

Only the cords of fear that cause you pain can be severed. You can never sever the cords of love. In order to release a non-serving energetic cord, you need to learn the lesson from that cord and dissolve it. Whenever you are experiencing a flare-up of a chronic pain issue or a mysterious or intense physical pain, you can clear any non-serving energetic cords and experience angelic pain relief. When you consciously cut and release cords of pain and fear, you actually strengthen the cords of love. To follow are some notes on what cord cutting is, and is not.

Cord cutting is *not* painful or about shaming, judging, or re-traumatizing you.

Cord cutting is:

- Reclaiming your freedom, and freeing to both people involved
- Enhancing your light
- Affirming your magnificence
- Discovering a gem, gift, and blessing

If you feel your pain is connected with a non-serving energetic cord, you can access the steps to cord cutting in the appendix.

Finally, earth angel medicine, which is also contained in your aura, includes:

- Your unique gifts, talents, and skills
- The blueprint of your soul's mission
- Your intentions and desires
- Your life's experiences

As we've discussed, your aura is the fourth layer of your energetic body, and it contains four layers itself. Your angels maintain your aura as one of their jobs, but you have to remember to ask for their assistance. Regularly tending to your aura is a highly beneficial practice that can help you keep the channels of communication between you and your angels clear and strong.

Now, it's time to put all this knowledge to work for you as you learn how to engage with your angels to heal your pain using the four practices.

PRACTICE ONE

Renew Your Devotion

Chapter Nine

My Dark Night of the Soul

When you are going through a "dark night of the soul," it's hard to believe it will be a blessing. I'm so grateful mine only lasted less than a year, especially since one of my spiritual teachers said her dark night of the soul lasted for nine years.

Landing in a psychiatric hospital for 11 days was a sad and scary time in my life, but it was also the "opening" that led me to find my angels and begin my devotional practice of receiving their love. Let me first share some of the events that led to the hospital.

I met my soulmate two years after graduating from massage school. We fell in love quickly and were engaged two years later.

We had many ideals in common and shared a similar vision for our lives. We both wanted to get married, buy a house, and have two kids. We purchased our first home together, which was a dream come true for me because I never had one as a child. My family had moved from apartment to apartment, and I never felt settled. So this purchase was quite monumental for me.

A few months after we got married, my husband's father was diagnosed with lung cancer and passed away four short months later.

I will always remember the moment my father-in-law crossed over because even though I was not consciously aware of angels at the time, I could feel them there. I was immersed in the love and prayers of that sacred moment. I was so honored to be there to witness a peaceful death. My father-in-law's passing felt like real closure with all my husband's family gathered around him.

This was a very emotional experience for me because I did not get to say goodbye to my own father, who had died tragically. Witnessing my father-in-law's passing was incredibly sad and brought up many layers of grief for me that I hadn't realised were there inside my heart.

Unfortunately (depending on how you look at it), dealing with grief in an Irish Catholic family meant drinking, which is what we proceeded to do. Many of those days following my father-in-law's funeral are a blur due to the level and frequency of intoxication used to numb, buffer, and deny the pain.

At the time, I felt tremendous shame about using drugs and alcohol to numb and buffer, but now—because of my devotion to receiving from my angels—I have so much compassion for who I was back then. One reason I felt shame about my self-medicating behaviors was because I knew it just wasn't good for my body. Even though I know it's common to party in your mid-twenties and experiment with drugs, the shame and guilt I felt were from overindulging.

My husband and I loved going to concerts and would often overindulge. I knew in my heart that this behavior was not congruent with being a massage therapist and yoga teacher, not to mention the havoc it wreaks on your physical body. I truly wanted to live a clean and pure life like yoga presented, and I knew smoking, drinking, and doing drugs didn't fit with the yogic philosophy. However, many years of partying lay ahead until I found out I was pregnant with my first child.

Talk about storm energy—in just five years' time, we bought a home, got married, lost my father-in-law, and I got pregnant. The pregnancy abruptly ended my partying days, and I went from numbing the pain of the loss of my father-in-law by partying way too much to being pregnant and sober in just a few short weeks.

Pregnancy and sobriety went hand in hand and came easier than I expected. I made the decision to have a natural childbirth. I thought that birthing naturally would purify me and wash away my past "sins" of alcohol and drug use. I knew this pregnancy was a chance for me to take better care of my physical body as well as this baby growing inside me.

Opting for a natural birth also gave me a much-needed focus since I was no longer numbing and buffering with substances. I read a ton of books and was fully committed to birthing with no drugs. And I did it! After twenty-seven hours of natural labor, my daughter was born. She was perfectly healthy and beautiful.

The natural birthing process really opened my root chakra. Suppressed memories and fears from my childhood abuse and trauma began to surface. My first year of motherhood was really challenging, especially as I wrestled with the relationship with my own mom. I really wanted my daughter's childhood to be better than mine. Becoming a mom was such a tender time for me. But, as it turned out, I had trouble being vulnerable and asking for help. I often felt isolated and scared, but didn't know how to express it.

Additionally, I was unaware of the suppressed emotions my body was carrying. Shortly after my daughter was born, I developed a severe case of body itching. It was an unexplainable symptom that I later was able to relate to stress and anxiety being released from my body. At the time, I found relief from the itching with acupuncture.

After the acupuncture cleared my body itching, I realized the need to practice better self-care. I became re-devoted to my yoga practice for support. I love stretching, breathing, and emoting on the mat. Thankfully, my mat became a sanctuary of peace and relief for my body, mind, and soul. It was a deep lower back and hip pain that led me to begin my study of the chakra system.

There was one day in particular—several months before being admitted to the psychiatric hospital—that my back pain was so intense that I wasn't able to work. Relying on my strong-willed nature and my training as a massage therapist and yoga teacher, I decided I could heal this myself.

My first attempt to heal the pain on my own with relaxation, stretching, and deep breathing opened up a very deep childhood memory of abuse. I was freaked out because I didn't know what to do with this scary memory and the associated suppressed emotions of fear, shame, and anger.

My angels led me to study the chakras, and I quickly learned that we store fear in the root chakra, directly where my back pain was. Chakras, which I discuss in Part Two: Energy Body 101, helped me understand the body/mind/soul connection. So much of what I read about the chakras deeply resonated with me, and I fell in love with the chakra system. I attended a weekend workshop with chakra expert Anodea Judith, who gave me a framework to understand myself and the emotions that I was experiencing in my body while doing yoga. The wisdom of the chakra system enhanced my yoga practice.

Before I became devoted to my angels, I was devoted to healing my physical body. I loved the peace and presence that yoga, breath, and chakra work brought into my life. However, yoga and chakra work also seemed to bring suppressed emotions and memories to the surface. Many times during my yoga practice and relaxation time, I would remember sad or scary experiences from my past, and I had no idea how to properly process them.

The perfect storm was brewing. I was a new mom with past trauma surfacing, a fear of asking for help, and little emotional support. This, coupled with abruptly stopping nursing my daughter at ten months instead of weaning slowly and a handful of sleepless nights caused me to have a manic episode.

It was this manic episode that landed me in the psychiatric hospital for 11 days. The multiple layers of shame, anger, and fear I had suppressed for years were coming to the surface for me to see and heal.

The doctors could not explain what had happened, and so they diagnosed me with bipolar disorder. The doctors prescribed meds and therapy to support me and their diagnosis. However, in my heart, I knew this diagnosis was inaccurate, and I became determined to heal myself naturally. It took years for me to realize what I was suffering from was actually PTSD and not bipolar disorder.

I now understand that the emotional time after leaving the hospital—which included a deep depression, overeating to fill the void, beating myself up for being weak, and feeling ashamed about having to go to the hospital in the first place—was a *dark night of the soul.* At the time, I had no awareness of the terminology. I just knew it sucked, and I wanted to feel better, happier, and like myself again. Whatever that meant.

My dark night of the soul put me face-to-face with my suppressed emotions of grief, shame, and many of my fears. That shadow time revealed the need for tools and support to move through—and beyond—the pain of my childhood so that I could be present for my daughter. It took many moons and years of therapy for me to see my time in the psychiatric hospital as my opening, but it was. It was an opening to my angels and to living a more soulful and devoted life.

I slowly pulled out of my dark night of the soul by attending classes and workshops that made me happy. Thankfully, I found a group of soulful women and a new spiritual tool that helped me hear my angels: oracle cards.

My introduction to oracle cards in a meditation class opened my heart and mind to the unconditional love of Source. Every time I worked with angel oracle cards, I felt happy and alive. I soon bought my own angel oracle cards and started to pull daily readings.

I was grateful for new friends and new tools. The angel oracle cards reawakened my connection to Reiki energy, which I had studied during my massage training. I felt ready to take my Reiki practice to the next level and became a Reiki Master. Channeling Reiki felt like a true soul calling because I felt happy, calm, and alive when giving or receiving Reiki. Self-Reiki taught me the importance of a daily meditation practice.

As I devoted myself to a daily meditation practice—which included a guided angel meditation, self-Reiki, and angel oracle cards—I noticed how much calmer, happier, and more peaceful I felt.

Daily meditation with a focus on keeping my heart and mind open led me to my angels. Of course, there were still many more years and layers of healing before I fully devoted myself to receiving love from my angels every day.

Chapter Ten

What Does Devotion Mean?

Devotion is defined as having love, loyalty, and enthusiasm for a cause, an activity, or a person. In this book, devotion means making a commitment to receiving love from your angels. Devotion is a sacred promise you make to yourself to embody unconditional love. Devotion also means having loyalty to your sacred self-care and your earth angel medicine by keeping a consistent and ongoing connection to your angels.

I know that the word devotion has a religious connotation for some. I see the word devotion as sacred rather than religious. Saying, "I am devoted to receiving love from my angels," is coming from the energy of:

I am committed and devoted.

I promise to take excellent care of myself in all ways.

I am loving and loyal to myself first.

I am enthusiastic about receiving love from my angels.

The devotion is to yourself, your body, and your earth angel medicine.

Devotion is not about worship. Actually, the angels do not want to be worshipped. Devotion is about aligning with the Divine and sacred within you and around you. The angels and archangels have no attachments or agenda. They are purely in service to the Divine and in service to unconditional love.

Devotion is a step toward receiving more love from your angels, and it's also a practice.

Renewing your devotion is the first of the four practices because it is the foundation that supports you in relaxing your body and mind, releasing and leading with your heart, and receiving and trusting your intuition. The Renew Your Devotion practice is a sacred promise you make to yourself. It is a heartfelt commitment to receiving love from your angels, over and over again. You make this promise with the full awareness that, in all your humanness, you will break it.

You make this sacred promise, you devote yourself to receiving from the angels, and then you break that promise. Your angels want to normalize breaking the promise. Breaking the promise is being human, and your angels never judge your human experience. Your angels actually revere your courage to become embodied and to do the inner work and spiritual growth of healing your pain, evolving your soul, and awakening your earth angel medicine.

Breaking the Sacred Promise

When you experience anything other than love, like pain, anxiety, worry, stress, sadness, self-doubt, or trauma, you are breaking the promise. On the path of the earth angel, you understand that these issues in the tissues are soul-chosen challenges, struggles, and difficulties that invite spiritual growth, higher awareness, healing, and evolution. Your team of angels that are around you right now are devoted to you and your pain relief.

Your angels are devoted to your awakening, your healing, and your enlightenment. Your angels know that your pain is both a block and a blessing to receiving their love. Pain is a block because it slows the flow of your angels' love. Pain can also be a blessing because it is an entry point for your angels' love. Of course, the angels say you can learn through pain, but you learn more through peace.

All you have to do to receive more love from your angels is devote and re-devote yourself every day without beating yourself up when you lose the connection or when you forget. It is important to not berate or punish yourself when you experience the same pain or pattern again. Your angels have unlimited compassion for your human journey and never judge or shame you.

It's important to be gentle and compassionate with yourself when that pain pattern surfaces. Returning to the pattern of pain, worry, or anxiety is breaking the promise. The angels want to normalize getting triggered, breaking the sacred promise, and re-devoting yourself to your healing in a loving way.

There are plenty of triggers throughout the day that slow the flow of your angels' love. Your chronic issue flares up again, and the pain is back. Your partner, friend, or sibling says something that upsets you, someone cuts you off while driving home from work, or your kid is misbehaving at school. When you get triggered, you have broken the sacred promise.

Being gentle with yourself when you are in pain makes it easier to re-devote to receiving angel love.

For example, when I was first diagnosed with Crohn's disease, I had a strong emotional reaction to the diagnosis. I felt shame, sadness, and frustration. When my parts felt shame or anger about the diagnosis, I was breaking the promise.

These uncomfortable emotions led me to eat a trigger food that caused a flare-up. Eating trigger foods was also breaking the promise. I was devoted to receiving love from my angels and cherishing my body-soul connection, and then I ate food that triggered a flare-up. All totally normal. Anytime you experience pain or fear, you have broken the sacred promise of receiving love from your angels.

The Renew Your Devotion practice is simple for a reason. In the morning, you devote yourself. Then sometime (or many times) during the day, you break the promise. You may break the sacred promise of staying in the flow of your angels' love one hundred times a day or more. To reconnect, all you have to do is pause and re-devote. You can place your hands over your heart, the gateway of your angels' love, and say, "I'm devoted to receiving love from my angels." That's it!

Just being aware of your devotion to receiving from your angels minute by minute, moment by moment, and day by day will strengthen your connection to receiving their love and healing. Breaking the sacred promise is part of being human and releases the pressure to be perfect. You are meant to be human. You are light and you are shadow. Remember, your angels love you completely and know all of you. It's safe to be human, make mistakes, break the sacred promise, and re-devote yourself to receiving from your angels to heal your body.

The love you allow yourself to receive from your angels will heal your physical body, the sacred home of your soul.

As an earth angel, you are called to ground the Divine. You are meant to fully embrace your humanity and experience pain and the full range of emotions. You are also meant to bring the loving energy of the Divine into your human body and onto the earth. You are grounding the Divine each time you tend to your physical body and energy body through your daily devotional practice of receiving love from your angels.

Your daily devotional practice is your sacred self-care time where you consciously receive love from your angels. The steps to creating a daily devotional practice to heal your physical pain with angel love include a conscious choice to align with the Divine.

Your practice begins with setting a crystal-clear intention, or fuel.

Chapter Eleven

What Is Your Fuel?

Your fuel is your intention. Spiritual law states that *energy follows intention*. This means that your energy goes where your attention flows. A foundational aspect of receiving from your angels is intention because once you set your intention, your energy will attract the help of the angels. Energy transcends time and space. You can begin to receive love from your angels the instant you set your intention. Setting your fuel invites the angels of your intention into your aura.

Your fuel is how you want to feel as you move through your day. Your fuel invites angel energy into your body and energy field. Your fuel focuses your mind and creates space for angelic pain relief. The list of fuels is endless. Common earth angel fuels are:

- Peace
- Compassion
- Joy
- Love
- Faith
- Trust
- Calm
- Ease

In the highest truth, you are already that which you seek. Your soul already has peace, courage, love, compassion, joy, and trust.

The goal is to release the pain so you can receive your angels' love and renew your devotion. Every time you renew your devotion, you receive more of your earth angel medicine.

What Is Your Earth Angel Medicine?

Your earth angel medicine consists of your unique talents, gifts, and blessings that your soul has received through many lifetimes of healing and transformation. Your earth angel medicine is your wisdom, which is unique to you. No one else can share, teach, and heal exactly the way you can. Your earth angel medicine is intended for you to first heal your body. As you heal, you may be guided to share your medicine with others, and this takes tremendous courage.

For example, some of my earth angel medicine is relaxation, alchemy, and joy. Many earth angels have these same qualities and gifts, but will share them in completely incomparable and distinct ways based on their life experiences and specific issues.

Shadow of Your Fuel

The shadow of your fuel is the opposite energy of your intention. Typically it is the dark side, or restrictive side, of your positive fuel. Once you choose your fuel, the shadow of your fuel is likely to surface, which is a good sign that you are beginning to embody your fuel.

As a highly sensitive soul, it's common to shy away from or fear the shadow of certain fuels. You may fear being overwhelmed by the shadow of your fuel. The angels want to normalize this fear, and they invite you to focus on re-devoting to your fuel every time the shadow arises. As long as you are allowing your angels to guide your fuel choice, you are safe to face your shadow.

For example, if your fuel is peace, the shadow may be pain. Your intention is to receive peace; however, your pain parts may get louder. Once you choose peace as your fuel, you will immediately feel peace as the angels of peace surround you. The peace that the angels are sending you flows into your body and mind and rubs up against the pain. This friction causes the pain to surface so it can be released.

Although uncomfortable at times, the shadow of your fuel arising is actually a positive sign. The shadow of your fuel surfaces because anything that is not your fuel needs to emerge to heal. The shadow of your fuel emerges so that you can truly embody and radiate your fuel.

Choosing a fuel and then experiencing the shadow side of your fuel is what builds spiritual mastery. Spiritual mastery happens each time you break the sacred promise and re-devote. Spiritual mastery occurs when you move through the love-pain-love cycle. You choose love, you experience pain, and once again you choose love. This is the path of the earth angel: To keep facing your pain with the eyes of love. This is part of your personal ascension and the ascension of the planet.

Spiritual mastery is not about suffering, sacrifice, or martyrdom. It's about being brave and trusting that the universe is benevolent and loves you unconditionally. You have to trust that there is a lesson at the core of the pain that you are ready to heal. That is why it is essential to choose a fuel, be human and break the promise, and then re-devote.

The angels want to normalize this process for you and assure you that it does not mean you are going backward or doing it incorrectly. Actually, experiencing the shadow of your fuel means you are ready to transform that pain or issue. Remember, your angels are supporting your fuel choice, and your angels would never set you up to fail or fall. God and the angels' loving benevolence will never give you anything you cannot handle. Remember, the angels have your back.

Recognizing that you are both light and shadow is part of your evolution. Knowing that there is a shadow side of the high vibrational fuel builds your inner strength and courage. Trusting this process helps you make a mindful fuel choice that both challenges you to grow and elevates your consciousness.

Chapter Twelve

Your Daily Devotional Practice Tools

Your daily devotional practice is your spiritual practice. It is your commitment to receiving love from your angels every day that heals pain or any issue. Your daily devotional practice includes a set of tools you use to receive angelic pain relief. These tools may include, but are not limited to:

- Prayer
- Meditation
- Self-energy work
- Journaling
- Mindful movement
- Angel oracle cards

Your daily devotional practice is designed to help you:

- Tend to both your physical and energy body in equal measure.
- Provide self-care and healing to your parts in pain.
- Make space for your angels' love in your body.
- Deepen your devotion to yourself and your angels.
- Ground your soul into your body and onto the earth.

You cannot do this daily devotional practice wrong, except by not doing it. Your daily devotional practice is highly unique and individual to your needs. This spiritual practice is designed to be fluid and dynamic and will change as you grow and heal pain. The suggestions here are guidelines to support your body's ability to heal pain by receiving angel love.

Prayer. Prayer is a spiritual tool for healing and a heartfelt communication with the Divine. Prayer is an ancient practice of talking to the Divine and asking for your needs to be met. There is power and potency in reciting a prayer that has been repeated by many for thousands of years.

Although this is not a religious book, one prayer that I say daily is Hail Mary. I have a strong connection to Mother Mary and all aspects of the Divine Mother. The Hail Mary prayer comforts me and makes me feel connected to the loving Goddess energy within me. I have included archangel prayers within the steps of each practice that you can work with daily to open the flow of angel energy into your heart and mind.

Prayer is gratitude. It is important when you pray to keep your prayers affirmative. Pray as if it is already done. You want to say thank you for whatever you are asking. The energy of gratitude will raise your vibration and keep your heart and mind focused on the positive and what you already have. This gratitude and positivity brings a feeling of abundance, which further raises your vibration, making it easier to receive your angels' love.

If you are experiencing back pain, for example, here are some suggestions for what you can say:

"Thank you, angels, for healing all my back pain."

"Thank you, God and the angels, for relieving all the pain in my back today."

"Thank you for leading me to the best healing tool or medicine for my back today."

"Thank you for filling me with peace and good health at this very moment."

Prayer increases your faith. Faith is complete trust in someone or something. Affirmative prayer declares that your prayer is already answered. When you acknowledge that your prayer is already answered, you feel gratitude. Praying in gratitude increases your faith. Your increased faith strengthens your body/soul/angel connection, relieving pain.

Meditation. If prayer is asking, meditation is receiving. Meditation is defined by a medical dictionary as:

> *"Meditation is a practice of concentrated focus upon a sound, object, visualization, the breath, movement, or attention itself in order to increase awareness of the present moment, reduce stress, promote relaxation, and enhance personal and spiritual growth."* [1]

Meditation is focus. Meditation is not complicated or difficult. Of course, when you are in pain, whether it's physical or emotional, it can seem like the last thing you want to do is slow down and focus.

I was first introduced to meditation as part of my yoga teacher training. I was 21 years old and a little distracted with my personal life and my budding relationship with my soulmate. Yoga teacher training was on Saturdays at 8 AM. I would often stay out too late the night before and was pretty tired when I got to class. I loved the yoga stretches and instruction, but when it came to the meditation part, I would often fall asleep.

Of course, I thought, "I can't meditate," and had lots of thoughts and feelings about my meditation practice. I didn't commit to a daily practice of meditation for another seven years,

1. https://medical-dictionary.thefreedictionary.com/meditation

until I became a Reiki Master. The first meditation that changed my life was the loving kindness meditation developed by one of my Reiki teachers.

What first intrigued me was that I was able to stay awake—yay! The loving kindness meditation is a 27-minute guided meditation filled with gratitude, light, chakra, and body healing. This beautiful meditation helped me feel my soul, my heart, and my oneness with the Divine.

The loving kindness meditation was the opening that helped me trust that I could meditate. I soon began to commit to a daily meditation practice, which continues to evolve. Now, I love creating angel meditations that heal pain and help you receive love from your angels.

There are many different types of meditation. Silent meditation, mantra meditation, walking meditations, guided angel meditations, and more. I have been meditating every day for over 14 years, and the type of meditation that works the best for me has been guided angel meditations.

If you are anything like I was, and think you cannot meditate, give yourself some time to explore all your options. I promise you will find something that works just for you.

Self-Energy Work. As an earth angel, you can clear and protect your energy by taking time for self-energy work. Self-energy work includes taking time every day to receive healing and loving energy into your body. This healing energy can simply be the pure light of the angels. Each meditation in this book offers that type of receiving. Self-energy work may also include channeling healing energy into your body from a specific training where you received an attunement, such as Angel Reiki or Integrated Energy Therapy (IET).

Although it is not necessary to have any Reiki or IET training or attunements to receive love from your angels, I have observed with my clients and students that these energy empowerments increase their ability to receive more love from their angels. An energy healing training and attunement can also provide a framework to support your body's natural healing abilities. Your self-Reiki or self-IET can be part of your daily devotional practice and can easily be merged into the guided angel meditations from each practice in this book.

Journaling. Your angels are always guiding you to express yourself and give your pain a voice so it can heal. Taking time to journal your thoughts and feelings can help you release pain. Journaling also helps you glean insight and wisdom that is held in the depths of your pain. The act of writing is grounding and brings you into the present moment so your angels can tend to your pain. Giving your pain parts a chance to express themselves and be heard is a powerful form of release. Journaling also increases and clarifies your intuition.

Mindful Movement. Your body was made to move. Making time each day to nourish your muscles, joints, and organs with mindful movement will not only help you hear your angels, but will release the stagnation that causes some pain. Your body knows what form of movement it needs to release pain. Moving your body with care opens the flow of life force energy and increases your ability to hear the whispers of your angels. When choosing your mindful movement, listen to what eases the pain and invites your angels' loving support.

Mindful Movement ideas:

- Yoga
- Dance
- Tai Chi

- Qi Gong
- Walking
- Biking
- Swimming
- Cardio or strength training

Angel Oracle Cards. Angel oracle cards are a wonderful way to enhance your angelic connection. Oracle cards offer support, focus, and validation of your direct intuitive guidance, which further opens your heart and mind to your angels' compassion. I love working with angel oracle cards and have found them to be a very powerful tool in helping me to receive my angels' love. As such, I have written about angel oracle cards in much more detail in the next chapter.

How you choose to create your daily devotional practice is unique to you. This spiritual practice is your commitment to connecting with and receiving love from your angels everyday in whatever way makes sense for you in the present moment. The key is being consistent enough to make it a daily priority in order to heal pain, stay connected, and receive your angels' love.

Chapter Thirteen

Angel Oracle Cards

Angel oracle cards are a divination tool that helps you communicate with the Divine. Angel oracle cards are physical cards that have an angel image and message. They usually have a guidebook that offers a deeper message and meaning to each card.

All angel oracle cards are positive, uplifting, and healing. You are not going to get a scary or disempowering message from your angels or the oracle cards. Even if the message triggers a part of you, it will be gentle and supportive as that part comes up for healing. Oracle cards do not replace medical advice or your own direct guidance; they offer support and clarity to heal your pain.

Oracle cards bring me so much joy. I love being able to receive a clear and uplifting message from my angels using this divination tool. I was first introduced to oracle cards in a meditation class and fell in love with the energy, wisdom, and healing that the oracle cards opened for me. I soon became an avid collector of oracle decks.

Angel oracle cards:

- Are grounding.
- Focus your mind.
- Validate your intuition.
- Provide divine support.

Angel oracle cards are grounding. The simple act of holding the deck in your hands and shuffling the cards to receive a message can ground you in the present moment. This is incredibly valuable because the present moment is where all healing takes place and where your angels are right now. Once you are in the present moment, the oracle cards offer you a focus that opens your heart and mind to their loving presence.

Being able to focus your mind on your angels is priceless. Focusing your mind to stay in constant contact with your angels is a challenge for every earth angel. Oracle cards can offer that focus because they give you a visual reminder of the angel or angel message with which you are meant to align. Your unwavering focus on your angels is what will bring the pain relief and healing energy you need.

Your intuition is your direct line to the Divine. Your intuition is how your angels are communicating pain-relieving messages to you. Angel oracle cards can provide a clear way for you to trust your intuition and your angels' messages.

Earth angels strive to embody the Divine, but it is essential to remember you are not doing this alone. Working with angel oracle decks that have a focus on the archangels and other divine beings can offer spiritual support when your pain gets loud. If the issue in the tissue you are experiencing flares up, using oracle cards is like placing ice on a burn—instant relief. Working with angel oracle cards will empower your ability to receive healing and pain relief from your angels.

How to Use Oracle Cards for Pain Relief

Once you have purchased an angel oracle deck, you want to make a connection with the deck that's easy and authentic. Hold the whole deck in your hands and say a simple prayer, such as, "May this angel oracle deck be a blessing to me and the world." Oracle cards are sacred divination tools, and you want to keep them in a safe, dry, and clean space to help them maintain their high vibration.

To use your angel oracle cards, you can follow this simple three step method:

- Ask quantum questions
- Choose the card
- Interpret the message

There are many ways of working with your angel card deck. While there is no one right way for this process, the following method is designed to provide swift and efficient pain relief answers. Simply enjoy receiving loving, pain-relieving messages from your angels through the cards.

Steps to Pulling an Angel Card for Pain Relief

1. Hold your deck in one hand and fan your thumb across the top of the deck to clear the energy.
2. Knock on the deck 3–5 times to clear the energy.
3. Split the deck and place half of the deck in one hand and half of the deck in your other hand.
4. Ask your quantum or empowering question.
5. Begin to shuffle, placing each half of the deck on top of the other until you get the feeling to stop shuffling. (Note: Any card that jumps out of the deck is your card.)
6. Take the top card as angel guidance to your question.

There are countless different ways to shuffle and choose your cards. It's important to note that angel cards are not playing cards. You don't have to mix them up and it is not necessary to shuffle them by shoving them in between each other like you do with playing cards. You can simply keep dividing and placing one half of the deck on top of the other half until you are guided to stop and pick your card.

Shuffling in this way opens your clairsentience channel. You will know when to stop shuffling for a few reasons. Shuffle until:

1. You physically feel that the weight of each half of the deck has equalized. Once you place the deck back together, choose the top card.
2. A card jumps out.
3. There's a slight, subtle lift of the top card when you are shuffling.

Asking Oracle Cards Quantum Questions. Your angels absolutely want to give you answers to heal your pain. Quantum questions go beyond the logical mind and access the infinite field of all possibilities and divine solutions. The quantum field is the space outside of linear clock time and is timeless. Your angels live outside of time in the quantum field.

When you ask your angels a question, the answer to your question is not always linear. It is easier to receive the answer to your questions if you ask the question as if it is already answered. Quantum questions have you step into the present moment with gratitude as if the answer to your question has already been answered.

When you're in pain, it's common to ask your angels linear questions like, "Why am I still in pain?" or, "Why don't I feel better?" or even, "What can I do to heal this pain?" However, when you ask a high-vibrational quantum question, you open yourself to hearing and receiving your angels' answers with more ease. To do this, you can begin a quantum question with "How is it that...?"

For example, instead of asking the linear question, "Why do I still have painful cystic acne?" you can ask a quantum question, such as, "How is that my skin is completely clear of all cystic acne right now?"

A good quantum question to ask could be, "How is it that I am experiencing total pain relief right now?" If you ask a question and the card doesn't resonate, simply ask another question. You won't have bad luck if you put the card back and ask a clearer question. The only caveat to this is that you need to be aware of asking a question with certain expectations and repeatedly putting cards back until you hear what you want to hear.

The oracle cards are meant to build trust between you and your angels; they are not there to support self-doubt. Your angels want to share messages with you. The Divine would never deny you access to the unconditional love that is your birthright. If you get an oracle card and it doesn't resonate, that's okay. You may need to clarify or simplify your question.

Interpreting Angel Card Messages. There are different ways you can interpret messages from your angel cards. They include:

- Angel image and colors
- Key word, phrase, or prayer
- Guidebook info
- Intuitive guidance

Angel Image and Colors. Pay attention to the colors, what the angel is doing, and the imagery in the angel card you pull. Colors have a frequency and vibration that can offer healing, and it's important to note the colors you see and connect with on the card as well as the color schemes you notice if you pull multiple cards.

The imagery on the card also has a message including what the angel is "doing" on the card. Notice if the angel is sitting, standing, or flying. Notice if the angel is holding anything or if the angel's eyes are open or closed. A picture is worth a thousand words, so pay attention to the imagery as it opens your heart and mind.

Key Word, Phrase, or Prayer. The key word, phrase, or prayer on the card is often a clear message that conveys many levels of focus and support. Remember, the oracle card is designed to open the flow of love and healing energy to relieve your pain. Sometimes, the answer to your prayer is the message on the oracle card that brings instant relief and reassurance.

Other times, the key word will awaken your inner knowing or help you focus your mind on the blessing in the pain. If the angel card you are using has a specific prayer, you are meant to say that prayer throughout the day to keep the channels of love and light from your angels open.

Guidebook Info. The guidebook can offer a deeper understanding of the angel oracle card and contain more answers to your prayers. The guidebook is created to offer clarity and to support your own intuition. There are often key words or phrases in the guidebook that light the path of healing and pain relief, so notice your own feelings, inner knowing, and synchronicities when you read the angel messages. It's okay if you are brand new to this practice and you do not "feel" anything right away—just keep praying and moving forward. Overall, the messages from the angel oracle cards will be positive, uplifting, and healing in many ways.

Intuitive Messages. The oracle cards are designed to open your direct intuitive channels. When you pull the angel card, pay close attention to how you feel when you receive the card. Trust what you see, feel, hear, know, sense, and even smell while connecting with the energy and information from the card. The more you trust and follow the angels' pain relief guidance, the clearer your intuition will be.

Chapter Fourteen

Steps for Practice One: Renew Your Devotion

There are five steps for Practice One: Renew Your Devotion. Each step is designed to build on the previous step, including circling back to the beginning, or step 1. The five steps are:

Step 1: Invite the Archangels of Renew Your Devotion

Step 2: State Your Devotion

Step 3: Choose Your Fuel

Step 4: Your Daily Devotional Practice

Step 5: Break the Promise. Re-Devote. Go Back to Step 1.

Step 1: Invite the Archangels of Renew Your Devotion

In order for the archangels to enter your aura and offer pain relief, you need to ask for and invite their help. You can use any number of prayers to invite the archangels' loving support that roughly follow this model:

- Recite the Archangel Invitation
- Pause, breathe, and receive
- Express gratitude

The Archangel Invitation I created is designed to welcome the medicine of the archangels of Renew Your Devotion: Archangel Michael, Archangel Metatron, Archangel Ariel, and Archangel

Sandalphon. Each of these archangels carry a specific medicine, as follows:

Archangel Michael—Angel of Protection

- Courage, strength, and safety
- Cut cords of pain
- Reclaim your magnificence

Archangel Metatron—Angel of Source Connection

- Prioritize self-honesty
- Direct connection to the Divine
- Chakra clearing

Archangel Ariel—Angel of Your Soul's Mission

- Courage to live your soul's mission
- Compassion for pain
- Spiritual freedom

Archangel Sandalphon—Angel of Gentleness

- Gentleness
- Prayers delivered to the Divine
- Ground soul into body and earth star chakra

Here is my suggested invitation (feel free to change or modify the invitation to your specific needs):

> *"Thank you Archangel Michael, Archangel Metatron, Archangel Ariel, Archangel Sandalphon, and the angels of self-devotion for guiding and protecting me with your healing light. Thank you for renewing my devotion to receiving love from my angels to heal my body every day. I am willing to relax, release, and receive your love to heal this pain. I ask that the healing I receive today be shared with all my relations in all directions of time."*

After you recite the invitation, take three deep breaths. Pause and let yourself receive the archangels' loving presence into your body and any points of pain. It's common when you are first inviting the archangels into your space to feel uncertainty, self-doubt, or skepticism about receiving pain relief from the angels. Be gentle and patient with the process. Humans say practice makes perfect; the angels say practice makes better.

Alternatively, you may feel an immediate shift in your vibration and pain level during and after reciting the archangel invitation. Know that you are wholly safe and protected when you work with the archangels' unconditionally loving energy. This step eventually becomes part of the next step as you may include the archangel invitation in your daily devotional practice.

After receiving healing from the archangels, it's important to express gratitude for their loving energy. Thanking the archangels opens your heart and allows you to receive more loving pain relief. Gratitude is magnetic and increases your capacity to receive more love from your angels.

Step 2: State Your Devotion

Each time you recite the affirmation of devotion, you are affirming in your mind the conscious choice to receive your angels' love. Everyone is receiving love from their angels all the time. Therefore, the shift you are making to heal your pain—as an earth angel—is to receive love from your angels consciously.

This step, stating your devotion, includes the following aspects:

- Invite Archangel Michael
- Open your heart to your angels' love
- Align your mind with Divine mind
- Receive your angels' devotion for you

To invite Archangel Michael in this step, you can use the following:

Thank you, Archangel Michael, for bringing the medicine of courage, protection, and strength to me and into my aura. I invite Archangel Michael's supreme protection and shield of peace to help me clearly state my devotion to receiving love from my angels. Thank you for cutting the cords of fear and pain and for giving me the strength and courage to state my devotion. I allow Archangel Michael's royal purple light and the angels of courage, protection, and strength to surround me now.

After inviting Archangel Michael, it's time to state your devotion. A simple but effective example statement looks like this: *"I am devoted to receiving love from my angels."*

Saying, "I am devoted to receiving love from my angels," is a key that opens your heart to your angels' love. This affirmation is designed to expand your ability to receive more love from the angelic realm. Remember, your heart is the gateway to your angels' love. Your open heart creates space for the unlimited compassion and unconditional love of the Divine to flow into your body and bring pain relief.

This affirmation aligns your consciousness with the love the angels are already sending to you. It opens the gateway and channels of receiving love from your angels. Stating your devotion aligns your mind with Divine mind, bringing divine solutions, miracles, and pain relief beyond your human consciousness, and at the same time directly through your consciousness.

The simple affirmation opens your heart and mind to receive your angels' devotion for your healing. It allows you to bathe in your angels' devotion for you. When you give yourself permission to receive your angels' devotion for you, your angelic connection strengthens. This strong connection makes it easier to stay open to the streams of endless love and light available for you, which provides angelic pain relief.

The affirmation is meant to be said many times throughout the day to keep you in the steady flow of your angels' love. You can say this affirmation any time you are feeling pain or a part of you feels triggered. Once you have been using this affirmation for some time, you can upgrade the affirmation to include your fuel:

"I am devoted to receiving (insert your fuel) from my angels."

Step 3: Choose Your Fuel

Your fuel is how you want to feel as you move through your day. Choosing your fuel is asking for what you want. It is your birthright to align with your highest intention of peace, compassion, joy, healing, unconditional love, and pain relief. The list of divine energies to embody and cultivate are endless.

Choosing your fuel involves the following aspects:

- Invite Archangel Metatron
- Self-honesty
- Choose how you want to feel
- Stay devoted to your fuel, even when shadow arises

To invite Archangel Metatron in this step, you can use the following:

> *Thank you, Archangel Metatron, for bringing the medicine of Source connection, chakra clearing, and prioritizing self-honesty to me and into my aura. I invite Archangel Metatron's loving presence and watermelon light to help me put myself first so I can honestly choose the highest vibrational fuel. Thank you for clearing my chakras with your cube of healing light, creating clarity and Source connection. I allow the angels of Source light, clarity, and prioritizing self-honesty to surround me now.*

Self-honesty is key to working with the angels. My teacher, Kyle Gray, says you have to first hear yourself before you can hear the angels. Being honest with yourself about how you feel in this moment will bring you closer to receiving love from your angels.

It is essential to be clear on how you feel right now. All of your feelings are welcomed by your angels. You can choose your fuel by deciphering exactly how you feel at this moment. Your feelings, just like your pain, are the entry points for angel love.

The moment you choose your fuel, the angels of that intentional fuel begin to surround and support you. If you choose peace, the angels of peace begin to infuse you with peace. This is a validation of your intention. This simple truth goes along with one of my mottos: *"There's an angel for that!"*

Choosing a fuel is an intuitive and divinely-led process. You want your soul to choose the fuel as guided by your angels, not your ego or your manager parts. Remember, your fuel is how you want to feel, and you get to choose how you feel.

The pain you are trying to release may have many layers. It can take time for the fuel you choose to become anchored in your physical body. Once you choose a fuel, keep devoting to that fuel for at least a week. Changing fuels daily can actually drain you because it can take a week or two to anchor or embody your soul-chosen fuel. Sometimes, embodying a fuel can take a lifetime.

When you are in pain—physically or emotionally—it's easy to worry about the issue in the tissue rather than focus on the healing goal. Embodying your fuel is the healing goal, and this takes courage, focus, and a willingness to feel the shadow side of your fuel. It's important to recognize that when you choose your fuel, the opposing energy or the shadow of that fuel can often get triggered. This is totally normal; the shadow coming to the surface for healing is actually a sign of your spiritual growth. When choosing your fuel, think K.I.S.S: Keep It Simple and Sacred.

Step 4: Your Daily Devotional Practice

The key to receiving a constant flow of your angels' love, no matter what type of pain you are experiencing, is to have a steady, consistent, and ongoing daily devotional practice. This means you do this practice—that you create—every single day.

Your daily devotional practice, or step four, is integral to your healing, and it includes the following elements:

- Invite Archangel Ariel
- Choose the same time for your daily practice
- Spiritual tools that help you relax, release, and receive
- Make it authentic to you and your lifestyle

To invite Archangel Ariel in this step, you can use the following:

Thank you, Archangel Ariel, for bringing the medicine of compassion, courage, and spiritual freedom to me and into my aura. I invite Archangel Ariel's courage to support me in staying devoted to my daily devotional practice and soul's mission. Thank you for filling me with your unconditional compassion and giving me the spiritual freedom to choose the tools that will serve my authentic expression. I allow Archangel Ariel's golden light and the angels of compassion, courage, and freedom to surround me now.

Your daily devotional practice can absolutely change from day to day, week to week, and month to month; it is meant to be fluid and dynamic. However, in order to receive the maximum benefit from your practice—which means the most love and angelic pain relief—it needs to be every day. The length of time doesn't matter and can vary from day to day. What matters is the daily devotion of receiving love from your angels.

Although you can absolutely do your daily devotional practice any time of day, my clients and I have found that doing your practice in the morning sets the intention and foundation for the flow of your day. Your daily devotional practice is an easy morning routine that includes relaxing, releasing, and receiving using spiritual tools.

You want your practice to include spiritual tools that open your heart to the angels. The spiritual tools you can use to receive love from your angels include, but are not limited to: prayer, journaling, meditation, self-energy work, oracle cards, and moving your body in a beautiful way, like yoga, dance, Tai Chi, Qi Gong, cardio, and nature walks. This is spiritual self-care, and the angels call it your daily devotional practice.

It's important to honor what you are already doing right now for your spiritual self-care. If you are brand new to this, it's all good. You can be in a beginner's mind and start where you are. It's important to create a devotional practice that is authentic to you.

There is no one right way to do this practice. The most important thing is that you let your soul and your angels lead. Your daily devotional practice has to fit into your life, wherever you are now. Your angels will always meet you where you are with compassion.

Your devotion or commitment to your daily devotional practice is more important than which specific tools you use. Each tool you engage in needs to feel supportive, loving, and even fun or joyful. This practice is flowing, alive, and aspires to awaken your earth angel medicine. Although repetition is important for integration, you want to make sure your practice does not become rote or stagnant. You are always being guided by your angels to grow, stretch, and evolve, and that includes your daily devotional practice.

Some earth angels can resist having a consistent daily devotional practice if any past lives included unnecessary solitude, celibacy, and strict spiritual practices that drained life instead of enhancing earthly experience. You can work with your angels and

Archangel Ariel to release this resistance to your daily devotional practice and find the right fit for you.

Step 5: Break the Sacred Promise and Re-Devote. Back to Step 1.

It is totally normal to be feeling good after devoting yourself to receiving your angels' love, and then get triggered. Being triggered or breaking the sacred promise means you are out of the flow of your angels' love.

Your healing journey is not about never being in pain or getting triggered. You are on a human journey, and getting triggered is how you build spiritual mastery as you move through the love-pain-love cycle. The path of the earth angel is about devoting and re-devoting to receive all the pain-relieving love you need.

This step of breaking the promise and re-devoting yourself asks you to:

- Invite Archangel Sandalphon
- Recognize you are triggered
- Pause, breathe, and place your hands over your heart
- Re-devote. Say silently or out loud: "I am devoted to receiving love from my angels."

To invite Archangel Sandalphon in this step, you can use the following:

Thank you, Archangel Sandalphon, for bringing the medicine of gentleness, grounding, and self-devotion to me and into my aura. I invite Archangel Sandalphon's gentleness to support me when I am in pain and have broken the sacred promise of receiving angelic love. Thank you for helping me ground my soul into my body and my body to the earth so I can re-devote with gentleness. I allow Archangel Sandalphon's turquoise light and the angels of gentleness, grounding, and self-devotion to surround me now.

Your angels want to normalize breaking the sacred promise and invite you to simply re-devote. Breaking the promise of receiving love from your angels can happen once to one hundred times in a day. There is no reason to beat yourself up; beating yourself up is breaking the promise again. Breaking the promise means you have stopped, blocked, or slowed the flow of receiving your angels' love in this moment, and pain or fear has returned.

To restore the flow, all you need to do is recognize that you have broken the promise and re-devote. Devotion is not about perfection; it's about commitment. You are devoted to receiving love from your angels, over and over again. Devotion is both a commitment to receiving your angels' love, which releases physical pain, and consciously releasing physical pain to receive more angelic love.

Once you realize you are triggered, you want to pause and breathe. Taking three deep breaths helps you slow down and re-devote. Next, place your hands over your heart, which is the gateway to your angels' love, and say silently or out loud, "I am devoted to receiving love from my angels." It can be helpful to say this two or three times, or until you feel a shift in your pain or anxiety level.

Renewing your devotion is the foundation that prepares you to relax, release, and receive.

- Relax your body and mind. A relaxed mind hears the Divine.
- Release the issue in the tissue. Let go of any layer of that pain.
- Receive your angels' love. Open, allow, and take in your angels' love.

Chapter Fifteen

Renew Your Devotion: Guided Angel Meditation

Each practice has its own guided angel meditation to support and reinforce the practice itself as well as your connection to your angels. By using these guided angel meditations, you open yourself to receiving more of your angels' love to heal your pain.

Begin with your breath. Inhale deeply and exhale completely, relaxing your shoulders as you exhale. Thank your body for serving you so well, and feel your soul inside of your body. As you breathe, feel the vastness and love of your soul expand outside of your body, into your aura, and up toward your angels. Feel your soul and your angels holding all of you. All of your parts are welcome.

Renew your Devotion. Gently bring your hands over your heart, the gateway of your angels' love and say silently or out loud, "I am devoted to receiving from my angels." Open your heart to your angels' love. Align your mind with Divine mind, and receive your angels' devotion for you.

Invite all your angels, guardian angels, allies, beloved ancestors, and the Archangels of Renew your Devotion—

Archangel Michael, the angel of protection; Archangel Ariel, the angel of your soul's mission; Archangel Sandalphon, the angel of gentleness and your earth star chakra; and Archangel Metatron, the angel of Source connection and your stellar gateway chakra. Invite the light of God, Source, Creator, Creatrix, and all the healing angels to be here now. Say, "Thank you for guiding and protecting me with your healing light for my highest good. I am the keeper of my mind and body and invite only those angels and guides that love me unconditionally."

Relax and cherish your body. Give yourself permission to fully relax and trust you are exactly where you are meant to be. As you breathe, welcome physical relaxation as you soften your muscles from your bones, releasing tension from your body. As you breathe, welcome emotional relaxation as your guardian angels make room for all of your feelings, emotions, and parts. Welcome mental relaxation as you slow down your thoughts. Gently focus on your breath and notice the space between your thoughts where all creativity, divine solutions, your intuition, and miracles reside opening your chakras. As you breathe, welcome spiritual relaxation as you surrender into the arms of your angels and expand your auric field. Trust the benevolent divine plan unfolding for your highest good and for all those you love.

As you breathe, send roots of light through your legs and out of the soles of your feet, into your earth star chakra and deep into the heart of the earth. Trust the wisdom of your roots to connect with the perfect crystals, tree roots, and ancestor medicine for you today, helping you release and receive more.

With your roots deep in the earth, welcome the Archangels of Renew Your Devotion and allow them full access to your body, mind, and emotions so you can deepen your self-compassion and your devotion to yourself.

Say, "I am devoted to receiving love from my angels." Align your consciousness with the love the angels are already sending you.

As you breathe, Invite Archangel Michael, the protector angel, to step forward with his sword of truth and cut the cords of fear, pain, self-abuse, and self-sabotage that are blocking you from stating your devotion. Receive Archangel Michael's strength and courage to cut the cords of pain and fear from your body and mind, leaving only cords of love. Say, "Thank you Archangel Michael for helping me feel safe and spiritually protected in all directions of time."

Once more, say, "I am devoted to receiving love from my angels," and align your mind with Divine mind.

As you breathe, invite Archangel Metatron, the angel of your stellar gateway chakra, to look into the depths of your soul, filling you with Source love. As you breathe, feel Archangel Metatron's loving presence awaken your soul's unique energetic signature, allowing you to be completely honest with yourself so you can choose your highest vibrational fuel. Receive the angelic pain relief of Metatron's cube—a glowing ball of healing light and sacred geometric shapes—flowing down your chakra channel, helping you prioritize yourself and release the shadow of your fuel.

Say, "I am devoted to receiving love from my angels," and open your heart to your angels' love.

As you breathe, invite Archangel Ariel, the angel of your soul's mission, to light up your soul. Breathe as you bring the light of your soul into your body and release the addiction to pain, suffering, worry, and self-abuse. As you breathe, welcome Archangel Ariel's heart medicine of deep compassion and spiritual freedom for your pain relief journey into your body, transforming all blocks to self-love and self-devotion. Invite Archangel Ariel's loving light to support your daily devotional practice of receiving love from your angels.

Say, "I am devoted to receiving love from my angels," and receive your angels' deep devotion for you and your healing.

As you breathe, invite Archangel Sandalphon, the angel of gentleness and your earth star chakra to help you tend to any parts that are triggered. Archangel Sandalphon gently touches the tops of your feet, activating your earth star chakra and strengthening your angelic connection after you break the sacred promise. Breathe and receive pure gentleness and gratitude into your muscles, bones, and cells, deep into your roots so you can re-devote with ease. Receive Archangel Sandalphon's complete devotion to your healing pain relief journey.

Release and lead with your heart. As you breathe, feel the Archangels of Renew Your Devotion clear your aura, releasing fear, pain, trauma, and any issue in the tissue that's blocking you from re-devoting to making yourself your highest priority. Each and every time you break the promise of self-devotion, be ever so gentle with yourself. Then place your hands over your heart, the gateway of your angels' love, and say, "I am devoted to receiving love from my angels." You are safe to release, release, release.

Receive and trust your intuition. Trust that your angels are always communicating with you through your psychic senses. Receive all of the love, compassion, and devotion you need to open your intuition. Trust what you see, feel, hear, know, sense, and smell in this sacred moment in time. Say, "Thank you angels for drawing near at this time and for revealing to me what I most need to know." You are safe to receive, receive, receive.

Receive a final blessing of pure gentleness, self-compassion, and gratitude from all of your healing angels and the Archangels of Renew Your Devotion.

Say, "I ask that the healing I receive today be shared with all my relations in all directions of time."

Take a cleansing breath in and out. Gently bring your hands into prayer mudra (position) as you bow to your soul and your loving angels, feeling your angels bow to you with love, devotion, and deep compassion. Seal your meditation with a Namaste (or an Amen, or other word you prefer).

PRACTICE TWO

Relax and Cherish Your Body

Chapter Sixteen

Pain as a Changemaker

Pain led me to become the Angel Professional I am today. Tearing my shoulder tendon was a blessing in disguise. The pain and inflammation I experienced had me re-evaluate how I was serving the world, my family, and my soul's mission.

Being a massage therapist was definitely part of my soul's mission. For almost 20 years, I was deeply devoted to helping my clients relax and feel better through the healing art of massage therapy. I loved the quiet and peaceful time during massages when I could just focus on my breath, the music, and relaxing my clients' muscles. In the second half of my massage career, I was also channeling Reiki and IET and calling on my clients' angels while I massaged them. It was a sacred and relaxing experience for me and my clients.

Once I tore my shoulder tendon, giving massages was no longer sustainable. My firsthand experience with pain allowed me to offer expert pain relief, but I was not cherishing my body by massaging others while in pain. I needed to listen to the wisdom of my body and the whispers of my angels. I needed to evolve how I served.

It was time to slow down and practice cherishing my body and give myself the gift of relaxation I offered my clients. The intense shoulder pain I experienced led me to explore the idea of retiring from my beloved massage career. However, it was tearing my ACL—and then my shoulder—that led me to deepen my connection to my earth angel medicine and ultimately leave my massage career.

It was a beautiful, sunny afternoon in the spring of 2015. My daughter was attending an after-school program at our parish. My son wanted to play at the park, and we invited his cousins to join. While the boys played, I was chatting with my husband on the phone. I noticed my toddler nephew was a good distance away from any adults. Within minutes, I found myself chasing after my nephew. To protect him from running into the street, I used my body as a shield and subsequently tore my ACL.

Let me back up a bit and share my mindset just before this accident. The weeks and months leading up to tearing my ACL were filled with stress, tension, and the odd feeling that a big change was about to occur.

I had a strong desire to become a spiritual teacher. I prayed about it everyday. It was a dream of mine to share spiritual truths and teachings and help people heal. Intuitively, I desired to make more income from teaching about angels and yoga than from massages.

Slowly, my dreams were becoming a reality. Just days before I tore my ACL, I had landed a new yoga teaching position and a private yoga student. I was about to go from teaching one yoga class a week to teaching six classes a week. To be honest, I had a small fear that I would not be able to keep up with this schedule even though I had prayed for it. I even wondered, "What if I get hurt?"

Weeks before the ACL tear, my soul and my angels gently guided me to slow down and listen. But at the time, my manager parts kept pushing forward without pausing to receive my angels' guidance. Although I prayed and meditated everyday, I wasn't really relaxing my mind.

Moments before I took off running after my young nephew, I received a very direct and crystal-clear message from Archangel Metatron guiding me to "start walking toward your nephew." However, because my parts were filled with stress, self-doubt, and anxiety, I did not listen to this intuitive angel message. Instead of listening to my angels, I ended up running after him—instead of walking, as directed—and tearing my ACL.

Immediately after I fell, I started praying to Archangel Raphael, the healer angel, and asked what I needed to do. A nice woman from the church got me some ice. I began to massage my knee and channel Reiki and IET to release the intense pain and fear. After about 20 minutes, I was able to get up and walk to my car.

After several days of pain and swelling, I went for an MRI. During the exam, the doctor at the clinic was sure I tore my ACL. The doctor was surprised how little bruising and swelling were present, but I knew it was because of the massage and energy work I gave myself immediately after the fall.

This was my first MRI, and my parts felt scared, both of the experience and the results. Thankfully, I leaned into angel meditations and tools to stay calm and still during the imaging. The MRI showed that I tore my left ACL, and I needed reconstructive surgery.

The surgery and recovery process brought me a new level of compassion for all those who go under the knife, as well as a deeper respect and gratitude for my angel tools. This was my first surgery, and my parts were very nervous. I'm so glad I had all my angel tools to keep me calm and relaxed.

The surgery itself was pretty straightforward, except that during the surgery, the doctor found that my meniscus needed extra work. This doubled my non-weight bearing period of recovery from two weeks to four weeks.

During those four weeks when all I could do was rest, pray, and meditate, I was beyond grateful for my daily devotional practice of receiving from my angels, even before I called it that. My meditation, self-energy work, and oracle cards practice were saving graces during a truly painful, emotional, and stressful time.

When I finally surrendered to the fact that I was stuck in bed, I gave myself permission to relax. Surrendering to relaxation allowed me to receive divine downloads and clear angelic messages about my next steps. Each time I relaxed, I could hear, see, and feel the angels more clearly.

Longevity in a massage career is all about body mechanics. Massage comes from your core and lower body to support the shoulders and hands. Unfortunately, I returned to massage work before my knee and core were strong enough to handle giving massages again.

The continued post-surgery knee pain caused me to use more upper body and shoulder strength during massages. These poor body mechanics, when combined with the strain of carrying my massage table, eventually tore my right shoulder tendon. The pain and inflammation in my shoulder were excruciating at times. I often couldn't think straight, and of course, every massage I gave just re-injured it.

I remember driving to a client's house while talking to my husband on the phone. The pain in my shoulder was so intense that I found myself screaming at him. It was a defining moment for me because something had to change. I needed to slow down and cherish my body. I knew in my heart that my massage career was ending, as it was no longer sustainable.

I prayed for my next steps. Although I did not see the full road ahead, I was led by my angels to hire a business coach who helped me transform my individual-session massage practice into the angel coaching practice I have today.

The journey of ending my beloved massage career to become an Angel Professional was filled with lots of pain and fear. However, I had to cherish my body and trust the divine order of all these events. I was being called to practice what I was teaching and walk in faith that the angels had my back.

Your Body Is a Divination Tool

With the impending end of my massage career and a large dip in finances, I experienced an interesting reaction. The physical pain in my shoulder caused stress and worry to take over my consciousness. My shoulder pain was diagnosed as a tear in my bicep tendon and a minor labral tear. Thankfully, I did not need surgery on my shoulder, just physical therapy. However, the financial fears from leaving my 20-year massage career meant my parts were constantly worrying about money and my next steps.

My parts were stressing about how I was going to pay my bills, and I experienced ongoing anxiety that my previous career was ending before my new career as an Angel Professional had taken off.

This persistent worry caused a series of odd body reactions to the high levels of stress and anxiety I was feeling. My symptoms were similar to an anxiety attack. My mind would race and my body would tense up. My intense focus on the future took me out of the present moment, which increased my anxiety. With my mind so worried about the future, I wasn't cherishing my body's needs. I was ignoring my body to worry about an unknown future.

One morning after the kids went to school, I was stressing and worrying about money and how my new angel business was going to work. I would often pull oracle cards to ease my mind. While standing at my mantle near the front door with the oracle cards in my hand, I fainted and lost consciousness for a minute. I woke up on the floor with a bloody lip and the oracle cards spilled all around me.

After the fainting incident, the weird body symptoms continued. I developed alarm clock headaches that woke me up in the middle of the night. It was an excruciating pain in the top of my head that cascaded down the back of my neck and across the top of my shoulders, like someone was squeezing me to death. This pain was disturbing my sleep and affecting my nervous system.

Another strange symptom I experienced was feeling lightheaded, dizzy, or nauseous when I worried about the future. If I didn't sit down fast enough, close my eyes, and breathe, my knees would buckle. I would fall to the ground and my body would tremble, almost like I was having a seizure. Then it would pass. My body was showing me that my thoughts were not aligned with the Divine, and I was not trusting my angels.

The alarm clock headaches and dizzy spells continued until I went to the emergency room.

Thankfully, the CT scan revealed nothing serious. No tumors, brain issues, or neurological issues. I did discover that I have mild arthritis in my neck, which surprised me because I have no pain there.

These physical issues shook my faith and had me questioning my path. I remember having a moment of self-doubt, asking myself, "Am I on the right path? Is all this energy work not working?" Once we ruled out anything serious, I knew I needed to relax and receive some healing.

Acupuncture and energy work helped again. After several healing acupuncture sessions, my symptoms subsided. I was sleeping again, and the headaches and lightheadedness were gone. I was relieved that this issue in the tissue had cleared up.

It was clear that I needed to trust my body as a divination tool and lean into my angel tools and gifts, not throw them away. I knew firsthand that listening to—cherishing—my body was integral to my path.

Chapter Seventeen

Cherishing Your Physical Body

Your body is a truth teller. As an earth angel, your body is the divination tool that allows you complete access to the Divine. Your body is divine technology, meaning that your body is designed to receive your angels' love through your energy body. Your body is wise and knows what it needs to heal.

The angels chose the word *cherish* because it means to protect and care for someone or something with love. Cherishing your body is about respecting your body's innate wisdom. Your angels cherish your body as the gift and miracle that it is. Your angels honor your body's truthful wisdom and guide you to do the same.

From the angelic perspective, your physical body is the sacred and precious home of your soul. Your angels love your body unconditionally. Just as your angels are devoted to your soul's healing and enlightenment, so is your body devoted to carrying your soul's light and earth angel medicine.

Your body is devoted to you! Just like your angels are.

Your physical body is well mapped out by the scientific and medical communities. Each muscle, bone, and organ system has been illustrated and outlined all the way to the nucleus of the cell so you can better understand its purpose and function. The way your physical body operates and cooperates, from the musculoskeletal system, to each organ system, down to the nucleus of each cell, is a miracle. Your bones, muscles, organs, and cellular matrix are held together by the vastness of your soul.

Your soul's loving light is what gives you the breath of life. Your soul is inside your body, pumping your heart, and expands outside of your body into your aura. Your soul is what animates and gives life to your physical body.

Your body is a miracle. Your physical body is designed to carry your soul's light and your angels' love. If your body is in pain, this issue in the tissue is not a punishment or consequence of past negative experiences. Your body is wise and loves you unconditionally. Your body is not betraying or sabotaging you when it gets ill or injured, it just needs more love.

Each issue in the tissue is a soul lesson which supports the evolution of your earth angel medicine. Taking care of your physical body is one of your main goals in life because when you take care of your body, you are also tending to your soul. Tending to both your physical and energetic body as well as your earth angel sensitivities makes it easier to hear the whispers of your angels.

Your physical body and soul work together intimately to share your earth angel gifts. Your angels lovingly hold your soul as you tend to your body. Your body is the precious temple of your soul, and your angels will communicate with you through your body. Your receptivity to your angel's love will deepen your body-soul connection.

Your angels understand the importance of maintaining health and wellness in your physical body so that you can share more of your earth angel medicine. Once an issue in the tissue manifests physically, it takes time and patience to heal. As an earth angel, you can make room for miracles and complete healing of any issue in the tissue.

However, part of your soul's journey is to bring healing to your physical body, and this takes time and devotion. The issues in the tissues are portals to accessing earth angel medicine. In other words, when fear is ready to release, it shows up as pain. Pain is an entry point for angelic love.

Your angels can heal physical pain and issues in the tissues by accessing your energy body. Loving, nourishing, and cherishing your physical body and energy body opens the doorway to your angelic team. Your team of angels want you to receive your soul's joy while on earth. One way to experience your soul's joy is through conscious relaxation of your body and mind.

Cherishing your body is a practice that restores health and wellbeing and allows greater access to your angels' love and wisdom. One of the fastest ways to cherish your body is by flowing through the levels of relaxation, which will open the layers of your energy body to receive your angels' love.

Relaxation is the gateway to angelic pain relief.

Chapter Eighteen

The Four Levels of Relaxation

What is relaxation? Relaxation is defined as a feeling of refreshing tranquility and an absence of tension and worry. There are many misconceptions about relaxation, including that it is a way to escape from, numb, or buffer your pain. Conscious relaxation allows your angels access to your pain and is the gateway to angelic pain relief.

Relaxation is a gift you give to your body and mind that supports natural pain relief. Relaxation is not:

- Sleep
- An escape
- Spacing out or zoning out
- Denying your feelings
- Running from an issue
- Distracting you from pain or taking you away from more important things

Relaxation creates the space for you to breathe, feel, emote, and release whatever is blocking you from receiving love and messages from your angels. Relaxation is:

- An arrival to your heart, your body, and this sacred moment in time
- Cherishing your body and energy body

- Space to feel, to breathe, and to be
- Tuning in
- Coming into the present moment (which is where your angels reside, here and now)
- Honoring your feelings and emotions
- Creating space to look at an issue from the perspective of your angels

Conscious relaxation allows you to receive more love and healing from your angels. Let's explore the four levels of relaxation, which include:

- Physical
- Emotional
- Mental
- Spiritual

Physical Relaxation. The first level of relaxation is physical relaxation. Physical relaxation is consciously relaxing your muscles from your bones. This level of relaxation helps you release tension built up in your body that can slow the flow of your angels' love. Conscious physical relaxation feeds your muscles and organs not only with fresh blood and oxygen, but with healing energy that will release toxins that cause pain.

Your angels' mission is to cherish you and guide you to cherish your body through this first level of relaxation. Your body instantly responds to fear or love in the physical layer.

Physical relaxation also includes sinking your energetic roots into the earth. Once you consciously relax your muscles from your bones, you can imagine sending your roots into the earth. Your energetic roots are a tool to release pain and toxins and to receive love and compassion both from the earth and the angels. When your body is physically relaxed, you can deepen and strengthen your connection to your roots.

Physical relaxation requires focus and loving attention on your physical body's needs and comfort in the present moment. Relaxing your physical body means making your body as comfortable as possible with the correct position and props that can allow your muscles and joints to soften and let go of tension. This loving attention is cherishing your body. Relaxing and cherishing your body relieves your pain and invites your angels' love to enter.

Emotional Relaxation. Emotional relaxation means there is room for all of you. There is space for all of your emotions, feelings, and parts. Your emotions are simply *energy in motion*. Your emotions are part of being human. There are no "good" or "bad" emotions. Every emotion has a lesson to teach and a gift to share. Your angels invite you to acknowledge, accept, and thank all your parts through emotional relaxation.

Emotions are magnetic. Your emotions magnetize and draw you to the people and situations with a similar vibration. This is not a judgment. There is no judgment from the angelic realm. Emotions are powerful and can become a source of anxiety if they are suppressed and not allowed to flow.

Your emotions are fueled by your thoughts. It is your parts inside that are having the thoughts and the feelings that cause pain. If your feelings are denied or suppressed, they become an issue for that part. Suppressed emotions may cause or be the source of physical pain.

Emotional relaxation is allowing your guardian angels to stretch your aura and make room for all of your parts to be seen, heard, and loved. When you release the resistance to the part and the emotion, your emotions calm. When your emotions calm and come into balance, your body relaxes even more. Remember, relaxation is the gateway to angelic pain relief.

Emotional relaxation means that no one part of you has to get really loud to be seen or heard. Your emotions are meant to inform you of your environment and be a source of inspiration. Other times, your emotions may also be a warning system. They can alert you to impending danger or warn you to be cautious. It's only when the emotions and parts get suppressed or denied that they get out of balance.

As an earth angel, it is important to honor the male and female energies within you. Emotional relaxation includes bringing both the masculine and feminine energies into harmony.

Masculine energy is connected to the right side of your body and is designed to:

- Give
- Take action
- Think logically
- Activate your willpower, clarity, and focus
- Harmonize the Yang (sun) energy

Feminine energy is connected to the left side of your body and is designed to:

- Receive
- Listen
- Allow intuition
- Nurture, comfort, and soothe
- Harmonize Yin (moon) energy

Emotional relaxation invites your emotions to flow naturally and allows your parts to have space to be seen and acknowledged. During the process of emotional relaxation, your body may twitch and shudder, and your emotions may rise and fall as you create space for your feelings. Knowing that your body may move involuntarily and that you may be shedding tears normalizes the experience. Acknowledging and accepting the natural flow of your emotions makes this a more gentle process.

There is a gem at the core of any difficult or challenging emotion. The depth of the pain you are experiencing allows that and even more peace to be experienced. Emotional relaxation is a safe process to feel your pain or sorrow and to allow the angels to transform it into peace.

Emotional relaxation often uncovers the source of physical pain in your body, and it can create deep relief, physically and emotionally. Your emotional intelligence and maturity increase exponentially when you make room to feel your pain. Allowing the pain and all the parts connected to it to be loved by your angels expands your earth angel medicine. It is a sign of spiritual strength to be able to feel your emotions and allow them to flow with grace.

Mental Relaxation. Mental relaxation is about slowing down and calming your monkey mind. Relaxing your mind is not about *no thought*, but rather creating space between your thoughts. The space between your thoughts is where miracles, divine solutions, creativity, and your intuition resides.

Your mind is designed to think. You have between 60,000 and 70,000 thoughts each day. Slowing your mind is no easy task. The simplest way to do this is to focus on your breath. Your breath is a powerful tool of transformation that can literally *change your mind.*

Mental relaxation takes the explicit awareness to *align your mind with Divine mind* and the willingness to let go of the thoughts that no longer serve you. Mental relaxation is not about controlling your thoughts, it's more about choosing a better or higher vibrational thought. Remember, your thoughts create your feelings, and your feelings are the magnet that draws the experience to you. *Positive thoughts create positive results.*

Mantra is a tool that supports mental relaxation, slowing down your thoughts and creating space for divine thought. Mantra means "tool of the mind," and is designed to focus your mind on a peaceful thought or on a sacred word or phrase. Mantras are not necessarily religious or about worshipping a deity, although many sacred mantras have some religious connections.

There is a mystical energy that surrounds certain mantras that have been chanted for thousands of years. When you chant an ancient mantra, like OM, you tap into the energetic vibration, support, and devotion of everyone who has ever chanted that mantra. There is healing power in the meaning and vibration of the sacred chant, as well as in the space it creates for angelic love to flow.

Repeating a positive affirmation, sacred word, or chant allows your mind to focus. This one focal point actually clears and calms your mind, allowing you to receive your angels' love and divine messages. *Your relaxed mind hears the Divine.*

Relaxing your mind is understanding that you choose your thoughts, not the other way around. Your thoughts do not choose you. You choose every single thought you have. When you think a thought over and over again, it becomes a belief. Spiritual mastery comes when you choose the thoughts that support your heart's true desire to achieve pain relief.

Taming your mind takes years of practice. Your angels encourage you to be gentle with those deeply rooted, ancient thoughts and beliefs that are stored in your mind and your chakras. Remember, your chakras are energy centers that both give and receive energy from the angels. Your chakras are angel receivers. You can access your chakra temples through mental relaxation.

A calm, conscious, and clear mind can help you access the high vibration of your chakras. Accessing your chakras is a heartfelt, intuitive process that requires a relaxed and open mind. The more relaxed your mind is, the deeper you can enter your chakra temple and receive the healing and pain relief your body needs.

Your chakras can be accessed through both the subconscious and conscious mind. In order to receive the full power and potency of each chakra's healing gifts, it's important to connect with your chakras through your conscious mind. Conscious contact with your chakras will open a clear portal to receiving the pain-relieving love and healing from the angels that your body needs.

Mental relaxation is about shifting from your overthinking mind into your intuitive feeling heart. Your heart is the gateway to your angels' love. Your angels guide you to relax your mind, which will sync your heart and mind. Although you need both your intellect and intuition to navigate human life, one aspect is not better than the other. Your goal is to bring your heart and mind into unison and have them work together.

Spiritual Relaxation. In one word, spiritual relaxation means surrender. From the angelic perspective, surrender is allowing your angels to support you in relaxing and cherishing your body, mind, and soul without fear or tension. Surrender means letting go of control, pain, and anxiety to go with the flow. Surrender invites deeper levels of unconditional love, compassion, and relaxation, which allows you to cherish your body.

Your painful parts may resist spiritual relaxation because it can feel like giving up. Giving up comes from victim consciousness and stems from feeling unworthy. Surrender does not mean giving up; it means letting go of pushing, striving, and rushing. Surrender is wisdom in action. Spiritual relaxation is practicing non-resistance and allowing your angels to provide swift pain relief.

Spiritual relaxation means trusting in divine order even if your logical ego mind resists it. Trust is the firm belief in the reliability and truth of someone or something. Trusting that the universe is benevolent, unconditionally loving, and compassionate takes spiritual strength and maturity, especially if you have experienced pain or trauma. Divine order is looking past the illusion of pain and fear to the higher truth that everything is as it needs to be. Trusting that there is a divine plan unfolding for your highest good and highest healing creates space for miracles.

As an earth angel, divine order is trusting the call to rise above drama, fear, and worry, and to keep your heart and mind open to the path of least resistance. Divine order stems from the Creator's optimism and knowing that there is a win-win situation brewing, one with divine solutions that are fair for everyone involved. Trusting divine order washes away pain, regret, shame, victimhood, and brings a peace that surpasses understanding.

Spiritual relaxation invites a *spiritual maturity* that creates space for Source love and divine miracles to shine through any pain or issue in the tissue. As you spiritually mature, you allow room for your angels' love to transform your pain into peace and your stress into ease. Spiritual maturity is not about being better than anyone; rather, it is faith that we are all connected in oneness. It is recognizing your own divine worth and accepting divine order in your heart and mind.

It's important to not confuse spiritual relaxation with giving your power away. When you relax spiritually, you actually claim your full power as a divine soul living a human life. It is in reclaiming and aligning with your full power that you can surrender your deepest pain and wounds to the Divine for healing.

Spiritual relaxation takes great strength because you are finally ready to release the resistance to your pain. It also requires courage because you are willing to see the full range of the pain within and know there is a higher purpose to your pain. Understanding that there is a higher purpose to your pain can calm your anxiety and make space for angelic love and healing to be received.

Spiritual relaxation makes *space for grace* to flow into your body and aura, releasing any pain you are experiencing. As the grace and love of your angels flow into your body or issue in the tissue, your pain dissolves. Spiritual relaxation provides a cushion of gentleness to soften your pain and releases harshness that slows the flow of your angels' love. Each level of relaxation taps into a layer of the energy body. Spiritual relaxation creates energetic space to access the layers of your aura so the angels can provide long-lasting pain relief.

Chapter Nineteen

Steps for Practice Two: Relax and Cherish Your Body

There are five steps for Practice Two: Relax and Cherish Your Body. Each step is designed to build on the previous step, as follows:

Step 1: Intention and Invitation of the Archangels of Relax and Cherish Your Body

Step 2: Physical Relaxation to Access Your Body and Roots

Step 3: Emotional Relaxation to Access Your Parts

Step 4: Mental Relaxation to Access Your Chakras

Step 5: Spiritual Relaxation to Access Your Aura

Step 1: Choose Your Intention and Invite the Archangels of Relax and Cherish Your Body

Remember, energy follows intention. Choose how you want to feel so the angels of your intention surround you. Your intention, or fuel, becomes the anchor for you to receive angelic pain relief. In this step, you will:

- Choose your intention
- Recite Archangel Invitation
- Pause, breathe, and receive
- Express gratitude

The Archangel Invitation I created is designed to welcome the medicine of the archangels of Relax and Cherish Your Body:

Archangel Gabriel, Archangel Haniel, Archangel Raphael, and Archangel Raguel. Each of these archangels carry a specific medicine, as follows:

Archangel Gabriel—Angel of Nurturing

- Communication
- Nurturing and cherishing your body and inner child
- Creative self-expression

Archangel Haniel—Angel of Sensitivity

- Empath protector
- Clairsentience, intuition, and moon cycles
- Aura clearing and emotional healing

Archangel Raphael—Angel of Healing

- Divine physician
- All levels of healing
- Miracles and divine intervention

Archangel Raguel—Angel of Harmony

- Divine order
- Relationship harmony
- Clairsentience

In order for the archangels to enter your aura and offer pain relief, you need to ask for and invite their help. You can use any number of prayers to invite the archangels' loving support. The invitation below is designed to welcome the medicine of the archangels of Relax and Cherish Your Body. Feel free to change or modify the invitation.

Thank you Archangel Raphael, Archangel Gabriel, Archangel Haniel, and Archangel Raguel for guiding and protecting me with your healing light. Thank you for helping me physically, emotionally, mentally, and spiritually relax and cherish my body. Thank you for healing (state your personal intention or issue) today. I ask that the healing I receive today be shared with all my relations in all directions of time.

After you recite the invitation, take three deep breaths. Pause and let yourself receive the archangels' loving presence into your body and any points of pain. It's common when you are first inviting the archangels into your space to feel uncertainty, self-doubt, or skepticism about receiving pain relief from the angels. Be gentle and patient with the process. Humans say practice makes perfect; the angels say practice makes better.

Step 2: Physical Relaxation

Physical relaxation requires attention to your body's position. It's important to support your head, neck, and lower back with props. Although I highly recommend learning how to relax in multiple different positions, I suggest lying down in the beginning to teach your muscles how to soften and let go. Make sure to prop your body in a way that creates relief, especially for your lower back and neck. Allow your body to feel heavy and supported by the surface on which you are sitting or lying. This step, physical relaxation, includes the following aspects:

- Invite Archangel Gabriel
- Place your body in a comfortable and still position
- Breathe and consciously relax your muscles from your bones
- Sink your energetic roots into the earth

We start with inviting Archangel Gabriel:

Thank you, Archangel Gabriel, for bringing me the medicine of physical relaxation, self-nurturing, and clear communication. I invite Archangel Gabriel's relaxing and nurturing energy to infuse my physical body with golden healing light, releasing tension and pain from my body. Thank you for helping me relax and clearly communicate with my body. I allow the angels of physical relaxation, self-nurturing, and clear communication to surround me now.

In order to fully relax your body, you need to have an awareness of the discomfort or pain you may be feeling. If you are new to sitting with your pain or discomfort, be gentle with this process. Your breath is a powerful tool of transformation and is the entryway into your pain. Physical relaxation begins with the breath. You can use your breath to create space for your angels' love to flow.

Conscious breaths are a way to cherish your body and release physical tension from your muscles. Deepen your breath to make your body as comfortable as possible at this moment. As you start consciously relaxing your muscles from your bones, from your crown down to your feet, you can send your breath into each body part, inviting spaciousness.

Relaxing the big and small muscles in the front and back of your body will soften your pain and shift your focus toward receiving your angels' love. Physical relaxation will help you reclaim your wholeness and inner peace.

Once your body feels relaxed, you can visualize your energetic roots sinking into the earth. Visualizing your roots moving through your legs and feet, into your earth star chakra and down into the layers of the earth to the heart of Mother Earth. There is a special space in Mother Earth's heart just for you. Imagine your roots connecting with the medicine of the earth and be nourished. Remember, your roots are a tool for you to release pain and receive healing.

Step 3: Emotional Relaxation

Emotional relaxation is unconditional acceptance. It is space for all your emotions and pain parts to be seen, heard, and loved. Acceptance is the action of agreeing to receive something offered. Your angels invite you to receive what your emotion or pain part has to offer you. In this step, you will:

- Invite Archangel Haniel
- Accept and thank your pain part
- Invite masculine and feminine energies to balance
- Allow your angels to create space for your emotions/pain

We begin by inviting Archangel Haniel:

Thank you, Archangel Haniel, for bringing me the medicine of emotional relaxation, ease, and sensitivity. I invite Archangel Haniel's bluish-white light to infuse my emotions with ease and relaxation so I can honor my feelings. I invite Archangel Haniel's sensitivity to flow into my sacral and navel chakras, creating space to feel and heal. I allow the angels of emotional relaxation, ease, and sensitivity to surround me now.

Acceptance is acknowledging, allowing, and releasing resistance to the pain. Accepting your pain creates space for your pain to soften and be seen. Once your pain or issue is seen through the eyes of love and acceptance, your pain can calm and balance.

Thanking your pain may seem counterintuitive, but remember that pain is a teacher. Approaching your pain—whether it's physical or emotional—with the attitude of gratitude creates space for your angels' love to enter. When you allow your emotions to flow, no one part of you has to scream or get loud to be heard.

Expressing gratitude to your pain may feel difficult at times. It can take practice to focus on gratitude instead of trying to get rid of the pain. However, thanking your emotions or pain allows your parts to relax and receive love from your angels.

Emotional relaxation invites harmony, including balancing your masculine and feminine energies. When your own male and female energies are in balance, your emotions calm and your body relaxes even more. Take a deep breath in and out, and say silently or out loud, "Thank you angels for balancing my masculine and feminine energies."

Spaciousness is the gift of emotional relaxation. Creating space for your pain to be seen and heard makes room to cherish your body and all your parts. Simply welcome the angels of emotional relaxation to surround your pain in spaciousness. This spaciousness will make room for you to tend to your pain and discover the lesson in the issue.

As you relax emotionally, your body may twitch and shudder and emotions may rise and fall as you release. This is totally normal and can be a good sign you are letting go.

Step 4: Mental Relaxation

Your heart is the gateway to your angels' love. By giving your mind permission to be present in your heart, your shift from head to heart will open the flow of your angels' pain-relieving love. To do this, this step involves:

- Inviting Archangel Raphael
- Slowing down your thoughts with your breath
- Chanting three OMs and tuning in to your chakras
- Inviting your breath into the pain

To invite Archangel Raphael:

Thank you, Archangel Raphael, for bringing me the medicine of mental relaxation, healing, and calm. I invite

Archangel Raphael's green healing light to flow in between my thoughts, calming my mind and opening my chakras. I am willing to heal and release painful thoughts and make space for my intuition, healing miracles, and divine solutions to enter my mind and my chakra temples. I allow the angels of mental relaxation, healing, and calm to surround me now.

You can calm your mind by focusing on your breath. A simple yet effective breath exercise to slow your thoughts down is to follow the length of your breath to the top of your inhalation. Then follow the length of your breath to the bottom of your exhalation. Three to five repetitions of this breath exercise will begin to create the space between your thoughts that will allow your mind to relax and receive your angels' love.

To shift from your thinking mind to your feeling heart, place the palms of your hands over your heart and lengthen your exhalations. Inhale to a count of four, and then exhale to a count of six. Repeat this breathing pattern three to five times, or until you shift from your mind into your heart. Longer exhalations activate the parasympathetic nervous system, so you can rest and relax your mind.

Your chakras are angel receivers. Tuning in to your chakras can calm and clear your mind. A relaxed mind hears the Divine. Your chakras are entry points for angelic pain relief, and you can chant the mantra OM to access these energy centers. You may also use the breath of harmony, which includes equalizing your inhale and your exhale. It may take several rounds of breathing to harmonize the length of your inhalation and exhalation. Equalizing your inhales and exhales brings equanimity and easy access to your chakra temples.

You can also direct your breath into a body part or into your pain. Breathing into the pain softens the surrounding tissues, allowing the fresh blood and oxygen to be carried there. Your angels' healing medicine is carried on the waves of your breath and in the molecules of oxygen. Breathing deeply is always a healing choice that relaxes your mind and invites angelic pain relief.

Step 5: Spiritual Relaxation

Spiritual relaxation is an energetic process. It's a vibrational mindset that allows the energy of pain to release. Spiritual relaxation is surrender and may occur naturally after you physically, emotionally, and mentally relax. In this step, you will:

- Invite Archangel Raguel
- Surrender pain to your angels
- Trust divine timing
- Create space for grace in your aura

To invite Archangel Raguel:

Thank you, Archangel Raguel, for bringing me the medicine of spiritual relaxation, divine order, and harmony. I invite Archangel Raguel's sky blue light to infuse each layer of my aura with surrender, grace, and harmony so I can let go of pain and trust the benevolence of the angels. I allow the angels of spiritual relaxation, divine order, and harmony to infuse my aura with their healing light, allowing me to relax into the arms of my angels.

Surrender is the willingness to let go of your attachment or connection to the pain. Surrendering your pain to the angels happens through your intention. Surrendering your pain to the angels allows your angels access to your aura creating space for grace. Spiritual relaxation to surrender pain may look like:

- Visualizing your pain as a dark mass that you hand to Archangel Raguel

- Writing to your guardian angels about your pain
- Saying, "I am willing to surrender this pain to my angels"
- Imagining your pain dissolving from your body and aura into your guardian angels' heart

Spiritual relaxation involves trusting the divine plan that is unfolding. Earth angels are here to embody the benevolence of the Divine and to trust that you are safe and spiritually protected. When you believe you are safe and the universe is benevolent, you invite spiritual relaxation. This level of trust in unconditional love expands your aura and creates space to heal your pain.

Grace is God's gift to humanity. When you relax into the arms of your angels and surrender your pain, you naturally create space for grace to flow into your body and energy field. Grace has the power to relax your body, mind, and soul. Grace is always available. When you spiritually relax into the safety and unconditional love of the Divine, you can access grace for pain relief with ease.

Chapter Twenty

Relax and Cherish Your Body: Guided Angel Meditation

Each practice has its own guided angel meditation to support and reinforce the practice itself as well as your connection to your angels. By using these guided angel meditations, you open yourself to receiving more of your angels' love to heal your pain.

Begin with your breath. Inhale deeply and exhale completely, relaxing your shoulders as you exhale. Thank your body for serving you so well and feel your soul inside your body. As you breathe, feel the vastness and love of your soul expand outside of your body, into your aura, and up toward your angels. Feel your loving angels welcoming all your parts.

As you breathe, invite all of your angels, guardian angels, allies, beloved ancestors, and the archangels of Relax and Cherish Your Body: Archangel Gabriel, the nurturing angel; Archangel Haniel, the angel of sensitivity; Archangel Raphael, the healer angel; and Archangel Raguel, the angel of relationship harmony, to surround your body in healing light. Invite the light of God, Source, Creator, Creatrix, and all the healing angels to be here now. Say, "Thank you for guiding and protecting me with your healing light for my highest good and highest healing. I am the keeper of my mind and body, and I welcome only those angels and guides that love me unconditionally."

Renew your devotion. Silently say, "I am devoted to receiving love from my angels." Open your heart to your angels' love. "I am devoted to receiving love from my angels." Align your mind with Divine mind. "I am devoted to receiving love from my angels." Receive your angels' devotion for you.

Relax and cherish your body. As you breathe, welcome physical relaxation as you soften and relax your muscles from your bones and release tension from your body. Relax the muscles in your face, jaw, and senses. Feel Archangel Raphael, the divine physician, lightly touch the back of your neck at your vagus nerve, bringing your parasympathetic nervous system online, rest, and digest. Relax the front of your throat and the back of your neck. Relax across your shoulders and down your arms and hands like a waterfall, letting go of any pain or any burdens you are carrying.

As you breathe, relax down your back and spine, one nerve and one vertebrae at a time, into your belly. Your breath massages your inner organs, relaxing your lower back. Feel Archangel Gabriel, the nurturing angel, gently soothing and relaxing your sacrum, your pelvis, and your hips. Relaxing down your legs and knees, down your shins and calves into your ankles and feet. As you breathe, feel your root chakra open as you send roots of light through your legs and feet into your earth star chakra and deep into the heart of the earth. Feel Mother Earth receiving you.

Trust the wisdom of your roots to connect with all the medicine of the earth, the perfect crystals, tree roots, and ancestor medicine for you today, amplifying your ability to release more and receive more.

As you breathe, welcome emotional relaxation as you feel your guardian angels and Archangel Haniel, the angel of sensitivity, stretching your aura making room for all of you, all of your emotions, your feelings, and your parts. All of your parts are seen, heard, and held by your loving angels. Breathe into your belly and allow your emotions to come into balance. As your emotions calm, feel your body relax even more.

As you breathe, welcome mental relaxation and Archangel Raphael, the healer angel, to slow down your mind and gently focus on your breath. Gently follow the length of your breath to the top of your inhalation and follow the length of your breath to the bottom of your exhalation, deep into your belly. Feel your breath creating space between your thoughts where all creativity, divine solutions, your intuition, and miracles reside. Allow your breath to open and balance each chakra with the medicine of compassion.

As you breathe, welcome spiritual relaxation and Archangel Raguel, the angel of harmony and divine order, as you surrender into the arms of your angels and expand your auric field. Allow the wisdom of surrender to fill your cells with deep peace. Receive the compassionate love of your angels, sealing any energy leaks in your aura where you may have given your power away. Trust that there is a benevolent, loving, and compassionate divine plan unfolding for your highest good and highest healing and for everyone you love. Breathe deeply and make space for grace.

Release and lead with your heart. In this deep state of relaxation, allow any physical pain, emotional pain, mental pain, and spiritual pain or toxins to release from your body through your breath, down through your roots, and gently out of your muscles, bones, and cells through your chakras and aura toward the alchemy of your angels' love.

Trust that releasing happens in layers, and it's totally normal for your body to twitch or shudder and for your emotions to rise and fall as you release. Allow your heart and mind to sync and sense that you are safe to release and lead with your heart. You are safe to release, release, release.

Receive and trust your intuition. As you breathe, relax your body and mind even more deeply and let yourself receive all the love, healing, and gentleness you need. Trust that your angels are always communicating with you through your body and your psychic senses. Welcome the angels of intuition to bless each intuitive channel with compassion.

You are safe to trust what you see, feel, hear, know, sense, and smell in this sacred moment in time. Allow yourself to receive all of the love, compassion, relaxation, and miracles that you need to heal your beautiful body and to move forward courageously into sharing your earth angel medicine. You are safe to receive, receive, receive.

Receive a final blessing of gentleness, compassion, and grace from all of the Archangels of Relax and Cherish Your Body and your own guardian angels.

Say, "I ask that all the healing I receive today be shared with all my relations in all directions of time."

Take a cleansing breath in and out, and bring your hands to your heart in prayer mudra (position). Bow to your soul and your angels as you see them bow to you with love, devotion, and deep compassion. Seal your meditation with a Namaste (or an Amen, or other word you prefer).

PRACTICE THREE

Release and Lead With Your Heart

Chapter Twenty-one

Transforming Hurt Into Heart-Opening Love

As an earth angel, you have a deep inner knowledge that you have been here before. You know in your bones that you have lived other lives. Your angels gently remind you that your soul is eternal, and that you chose the details of your reincarnation. Each incarnation is a soul-chosen experience that helps your soul to grow, heal, and evolve. The more challenging the lessons, the more growth will occur.

Before you were born as the person you are today, you had a divine meeting with your angels and guides to choose your life. You chose your parents and family, you chose your birthdate and astrological sign, you even chose which patterns or karmas you wanted to heal and work on in this lifetime. Accepting that you chose these challenges and difficulties is a liberating concept because no one has power over you. Accepting that you chose each and every challenge, karma, and difficulty releases any blame or victimhood. Accepting your freedom to choose allows you to reclaim your personal power. You always have the free will to choose again.

The earth angels' mission is simple: Be a channel of unconditional love. Simple does not always mean easy, however. To be a channel of unconditional love means you will love everyone and love without condition. This is a tall order and one that takes lifetimes to fill. You don't just love what is easy to love, you are also called to love the "unlovable" shadow parts, too. Transforming the shadow into light is one of the many divine gifts your angels hope you receive.

Just as your soul chose your life circumstances, you also agreed to have *amnesia*. You agreed to forget that you chose and forget that you are one with the Divine. Life is a journey to remember who you are: a creative, loving, and powerful child of God. Every time you choose love over fear, your soul grows.

I write this story with the utmost compassion for myself, my parents, and my inner children. I accept full responsibility for the intense karmas I came here to heal in this lifetime. I am making the conscious choice not to blame my parents or my grandparents. Releasing blame awakens your inner strength and personal liberation.

The karmas of hurt, pain, shame, abuse, trauma, rescuing, excessive responsibility, and addictions were woven into the fabric of my DNA. I chose the perfect family and set of circumstances to heal these patterns not only for my own soul's growth, but also for my ancestors' souls. No mud, no lotus.

I pray that what I share here assists you in releasing your personal and ancestral hurts so you can lead with your big, beautiful heart.

I was born on November 23, 1978 to two parents who had many of their own issues in the tissues. Although this is not my parents' story, it's important to include the roots I was born into. This sets the stage for the many difficulties that I chose to experience and heal in this lifetime. Both my parents experienced their own personal horrors, including emotional abuse, mental illness, death by accidental overdose of a parent, addictions, and other trauma that led them to make unsupported decisions in the moment.

In one word, my childhood was chaos. Neither of my parents had emotional, familial, or financial support. They were forced to make it on their own. From my infancy, we lived in roach-infested apartments and moved almost every year. I probably lived in at least eight different apartments by the time I was ten years old. I went to six different grammar schools and never really felt settled or safe.

My parents were often stressed and fighting. Self-care was not a thing in my parents' lives. Instead, they engaged in unhealthy behaviors to manage their stress. The lack of support in their lives led them to make difficult choices, and this created immense emotional pain for each of us.

My childhood was riddled with scary and unstable situations, including being sexually and emotionally abused. I experienced familial violence, extreme stress, substance abuse, and poverty, which included being homeless and living in a car for a few months. Each of these experiences created micro-hurts that lodged in my heart.

Another soul-chosen karma for me in this lifetime has been the combination of excessive responsibility, the urge to rescue those around me, and shouldering the hurts and burdens of others. I experienced many opportunities to live out these karmas. When my parents were working or "unavailable," I often had to watch my younger brother. This need to be "in charge" and responsible at a young age diminished my innocence.

My only relief was nature. I felt at peace outside, swinging on the swing, riding my bike, or playing in the grass in the woods or near the lake. I rarely wanted to be home in the chaos. I would rather be outside where I could breathe and feel alive and free.

I also found solace in school and became a very good student. Even though I went to six different grammar schools, I always felt happy at school. It was organized, predictable, and mostly safe. Despite the constant family drama, I was a happy kid. I was cheerful and wanted to make others happy. Like most children, I wanted my parents' attention, and I would often listen to their woes and distresses to have a connection. I later realized I was absorbing the hurt and pain they felt like a sponge, adding to the micro-hurts in my heart.

I was an incredibly intuitive and sensitive child. I had a big heart for all animals, especially cats. I even thought my stuffed animals had feelings and never wanted them to be thrown or crumpled. Before I knew anything about past lives, I used to wonder what it would be like to see through someone else's eyes or live their life instead of my own. I often felt I had lived before, and I would receive intense déjà vu visions.

My sensitivity and my intuition were strong. My claircognizance was one of my stronger channels, even though I had no name for this ability to hear divine thought. I would often surprise the adults in the room by saying really wise and intelligent things. They would always say, "How did you know that?" I never knew the source of the knowledge, but I was certain it was the truth.

I remember having a thought that later haunted me and even produced tremendous guilt. The thought I had was, "What if I only had one parent?" For many years after my dad's death, I always felt like somehow it was maybe my fault he died, because of that thought. As an adult, I believe it was my angels preparing me for the tragic event that was to unfold.

The intensity and chaos I experienced as a child culminated in the huge heartbreak that turned all the tiny hurt pebbles into a mountain of hurt when my father was murdered.

In December of 1989, when I was 11 years old, my father was stabbed to death and died a hero. My dad was walking to the corner store (I'm sure to buy beer and cigarettes), when he saw an older gentleman being held up at knife point. My father stepped into the robbery and was stabbed in the heart and lungs. My father was very physically fit, and as such he had the strength to stumble home, which was about a block away. The robber followed him and slit his throat in the gangway of our apartment building.

By the grace of God and the angels, my brother and I were both spending a second night at our friends' house. We had tons of sleepovers, but we never spent two nights in a row. That night, both our parents agreed. The memory is pretty foggy, but I think I spoke with my dad on the phone that night. He sounded really sad. I had no idea it would be the last time I would speak to him.

Surely the angels spared my brother and I from seeing our father dead at the bottom of our staircase. As you can imagine, the traumatic death of my father created a mountain of hurt, anger, fear, and grief that was going to take a miracle to release.

Thankfully, miracles did occur after my dad died. My father's murder was a huge wake up call for my mom to take better care of herself, and she did. She put herself through nursing school, left waitressing, and became a registered nurse (RN). We lived in bigger, nicer, and cleaner apartments for longer lengths of time, which was comforting. I was able to attend one high school for all four years, which was a relief.

Our lives improved drastically when my mom practiced better self-care. She started using tarot cards to help her cope with her loss. She even tried different kinds of self-care techniques like yoga and the Five Tibetan Rites to manage the stress of being a single mom. "When you know better, you do better."

My mom had a lot to process and deal with after my dad died. She truly did the best she could to make our lives better after the trauma of his murder and our difficult childhood. My mom was extremely intuitive and a good listener. She allowed me the freedom to make my own choices and mistakes. She bought me my first car, a Hyundai, and paid for most of my massage school training. I am deeply grateful for my mom's courage and inner strength that kept the family together and made a better life for me and my brother.

After my traumatic and stressful childhood, I sought relaxation and relief. This desire to relax and be happy led me to become a massage therapist at 18 years old. I was inspired to go to massage school by my older half-brother, who was also a massage therapist. Instead of going to college as planned, I chose one of the best massage schools in Chicago directly out of high school. This bold move was the beginning of my healing journey.

My massage practice quickly led me to yoga. At 19 years old, I found the best massage job in Evanston. I worked in a cozy home studio with two massage rooms, a hot tub, and an Iyengar yoga studio with slings on the wall and a fireplace. The studio owner was a longtime massage therapist and yoga teacher.

I will never forget my first yoga class the summer I graduated from massage school. The room was packed because the teacher was leaving town the next day. The yoga class, which ended in the final relaxation pose, savasana, made me feel like I had just had a massage. I was hooked. My personal yoga practice led me to become a yoga teacher, and my yoga training led me to explore the chakras and energy work. My first Reiki attunement was during an elective class for massage school. Practicing yoga awakened my interest in the chakras and Reiki.

I didn't fully commit to my Reiki journey until several years later when I became a Reiki Master. I soon discovered new levels of the energy world, including my angels. My devotion to my daily meditation, self-Reiki, and oracle cards led me to Integrated Energy Therapy, or IET, and a deeper and more clear connection to my angels.

My soul's desire to be happy despite all of my painful childhood experiences created a deep connection to the Divine through the angelic realm. Through the process of releasing and leading with my heart, my angels taught me that remaining hurt is a choice. You can choose to be hurt by someone, or you can choose to release the hurt and keep leading with your tender heart.

Although the age old adage "hurt people, hurt people" is true on many levels, as a resilient and loving earth angel, you can choose to release the hurt, like water off a duck's back, and return to your loving heart again and again. Every time you choose love over fear, your ability to be a channel of unconditional love grows.

Chapter Twenty-two

What is Releasing?

What is Releasing? Releasing is defined as allowing something to move, act, or flow freely. Releasing is the ability to let go of what no longer serves you in a gentle way. Releasing is not rejecting your parts or having a strong aversion to the issue or wound. When you release with the angels, you let go with love and respect for how the pain served you. Releasing is a sacred and non-linear process that can trigger your ego parts. Conscious releasing may feel messy, emotional, and out of your control at times, but it is a necessary step to receive angelic pain relief.

Releasing is *not*:

- Rejecting pain
- Dumping pain on anyone
- Numbing or escaping
- Causing yourself or anyone else harm
- Getting rid of your parts

Releasing is:

- Simple, but not always easy
- Emptying out your pain
- Creating space in your body for your angels' love
- Letting go of what no longer serves you, even if it did serve you at one time

- Surrendering control
- Processing your emotions
- A conscious practice to effect a real change or create transformation

When a memory or pain arises, you are ready to see it differently. When suppressed pain surfaces, you are ready to learn the deeper lesson and turn this wound into wisdom.

Forms of release include:

- Body movement
- Crying
- Laughter
- Screaming
- Healing without feeling
- Through energy body, roots, chakras, and aura

Releasing happens in layers. It's totally normal for your body to twitch, shudder, or move involuntarily as you release. The angels want to normalize this for you. I remember shaking or trembling would happen to me while I relaxed during my yoga practice. In that state of relaxation, old trauma would surface and my body would respond to the painful memories by moving involuntarily. At first, it made me nervous. However, I felt better afterwards, so I knew I was on the right path. I kept trusting my body's truthful wisdom and my angels' love to support me.

Releasing suppressed pain can often evoke an emotional response. It is very common to cry, scream, or even laugh for a moment and then settle back down. If you have suppressed many layers of sadness or grief, it is quite common to cry a lot at first. You can always ask for the emotional release to be gentle, healing, and not overwhelming. Releasing suppressed grief can feel really good at first, then may start to feel draining. Remember to drink water and take it easy and slow.

Although screaming is not always a comfortable release, suppressed anger or fear may need to be released in that way. If you feel the need to have a guttural scream to release anger, grab a pillow and scream into it. Anger is the most difficult emotion for the human body to release once it is suppressed. Safe physical movements, including yoga, cardio, dancing, and even punching a pillow, are helpful ways to release suppressed anger.

Another form of emotional release is laughter. This is my favorite release, and I wish it happened more frequently because a good belly laugh is very healing. If you release through laughter, it can be just for a moment followed by more tears, or vice versa. Tears can turn into laughter when you let go of pain or trauma.

Some people experience *healing without feeling* and have little to no body movement or emotions. This is not as common amongst earth angels, who feel things so deeply, but it can happen. When you are devoted to consciously releasing pain, it will happen whether you feel anything or not.

Releasing is vulnerable, brave, and not for the faint of heart. It takes great courage to feel your pain (just a little) so your grateful heart can tenderly open once again. Conscious releasing of your pain creates space for your angels' love to flow into your body.

The Three Safety Nets of Releasing

There are three "safety nets" of releasing that will help you as you move through this process. These gifts from your angels and Source include:

- Cushions of comfort
- Release only when ready
- No rushing

Cushions of Comfort. Once you are ready to release, your angels begin to send you even more cushions of love, comfort, support, and compassion. This extra love bubble will soften the intensity of the suppressed pain and make it a gentler release. *You will never have to feel the full intensity or depth of the buried pain when you ask the angels for support.* You only feel a small fraction of it as part of the integration process. You will never get flooded with or drown in what you are releasing when you stay open to your angels' love.

Release Only When Ready. Another safety net from Source and your guardian angels is that you cannot release anything you are not ready to release. It kind of reminds me of the wise statement, *God doesn't give you anything you can't handle.* Your guardian angels know exactly what you are ready to release. Your angels also know to what level you can safely release while still staying grounded and open. Rest assured that if you are being guided to release pain, fear, anger, sadness, or trauma, you are ready!

If you experienced a traumatic incident, your guardian angels know that the pain may be too much for your consciousness to process at the time of the incident. The pain is suppressed until you are ready to process it. What triggers a seven-year-old may not trigger a 30-year-old. The trauma of my father's murder was too much for my 11-year-old heart and mind to handle. I buried the hurt, grief, and fear until I was an adult and a parent myself. Then my soul knew it was time for me to process and integrate the pain of that experience, and release it.

No Rushing. You can't rush your healing. Earth angels have a deep respect for divine order. Your angels' love is infinitely patient and unconditional and will never create a sense of urgency. Your angels invite you to be patient and will never push or rush the releasing process. If you feel rushed, that's a part pushing you, not your angels. It's important to have compassion for that part and to keep trusting divine timing. You can take all the time you need to release the pain with ease.

Chapter Twenty-three

Micro-Hurts, Pain, and Opening Your Heart

As the gateway to your angels' love, your heart is the fastest way for your angels to communicate with you. If your heart is filled with hurt, it creates a barrier to receiving your angels' love.

Micro-Hurts

Your angels liken the hurt in your heart to the image of a small pebble. When someone says or does something that hurts you, it creates a tiny pebble in your heart. The angels call these tiny pebbles *micro-hurts*.

You have two options to clear the micro-hurt. One option is to speak up to the person and clear the air. In that way, you dissolve the pebble. The second option is to forgive the transgression and release the grievance, thereby dissolving the pebble.

When you do not release the micro-hurt, the pebble eventually turns into a rock. This rock again creates a barrier that prevents you from receiving your angels' love and messages. If you do not consciously release the rock of hurt in your heart, you are likely to keep attracting similar hurts. This turns the rock into a boulder. Eventually, without conscious releasing, the heart boulder may turn into a mountain. This mountainous hurt in your heart creates a huge barrier to receiving angelic pain relief.

If the hurt in your heart becomes a mountain, it takes the extraordinary power of unconditional compassion and unconditional love to dissolve the mountain of hurt, allowing your heart to be open and tender once again.

When you have a boulder or a mountain of hurt in your heart, it can be challenging to lead with your heart. It's natural when your heart is hurting to avoid your heart space and default to using intellect and logic to move forward. Often, the heart boulder pressures you to use more of your mind's logic rather than your heart's intuitive power.

As an earth angel, you absolutely need your intellectual mind to navigate the earth plane, just like you need your parts. *Your heart's magnetism can train your mind to stay present in love so your heart can lead the way.* Your angels always guide you to sync your heart's intuitive power with your mind's logic for you to experience peace and wholeness.

Allowing the micro-hurts to turn into a boulder of hurt does not protect you from more hurt. Your parts may feel that holding on to the micro-hurts will protect you and keep you safe from more hurt. However, hurt attracts hurt, just like light attracts light. As you have learned, the hurt is a part. You cannot get rid of your hurt parts. However, you can pause and thank the hurt part for trying to protect you. Then you can invite your angels to surround the hurt part in love and compassion to help it release its pain.

The Depth of Your Pain

Your heart is the center of love as well as the center of your being, both physically and spiritually. Your heart is an alchemical space where miraculous and divine healing can occur. Your heart is the first source of unconditional love in your body. Unconditional love is the greatest power in the universe, and this great power is right in the center of your being.

Remember, your heart is also the gateway to your angels' love. The most direct way to receive your angels' love is through your heart. Your angels want you to pour your heart out to them. There is no judgment from the angelic realm. They are not judging your pain, your hurt, or your grief. The more you open your heart to your angels, the more love you can receive.

Your angels want to release all the micro-hurts and heart boulders that block the flow of their love. Your angels guide you to understand that there is no need to fear the depth of your pain because the angels can transform it into peace. *The depth of the pain you feel is equal to the depth of the peace you can receive.*

The deeper you feel the wound of hurt, the deeper and more profoundly you will feel and receive self-compassion. This is the angelic alchemy of transforming your wound into wisdom. The depth of the hurt you experience is equal to the depth of the compassion you can create.

When you open your grateful heart to your angels' love, you have the power to transform any pain or hurt into peace and compassion.

Open Your Grateful Heart

Gratitude magnetizes miracles. Miracles are simply a shift from fear to love. Miracles are natural and can move the mountain of hurt you have in your heart. Being thankful activates your heart to open more deeply to your angels' love. Your angels' love is what has the power to transform the hurt and pain into greater levels of compassion and wisdom.

The attitude of gratitude is the key to open the gateway to your heart's unconditional love. Gratitude is like the grease you put on the rusty hinges of the gate that leads to your heart's treasures. The micro-hurts in your heart are the rust on the hinges of the gate that slows the flow of your angels' love.

Choosing to be grateful for your blessings is one level of gratitude and a great place to start. Your spiritual mastery grows when you have the strength to be grateful for your challenges, issues, and pain. Being grateful for your struggles doesn't happen overnight, and you do not want to bypass or suppress your feelings. However, when you shift to the attitude of gratitude for the pain, the gateway of your heart flies open to receive more love from your angels.

Gratitude is also appreciation for yourself and your journey. *Self-appreciation creates a cushion of love around you that attracts more angels to your side.* When you appreciate yourself, this grateful energy magnetizes people and situations that mirror your self-appreciation. Self-appreciation invites you to cherish your body and release your pain so you can receive more love from your angels. Self-appreciation increases your ability to receive more compassion.

Release and Lead With Your Heart means having the willingness to release the hurt, grief, and pain in your heart and the courage to let your tender heart lead the way.

Sync Your Heart and Mind

Your heart is meant to lead you. *Your heart is the master teacher and your mind is the humble student.* Syncing your heart and mind is about intentionally aligning your intuition and your intellect. You need both your heart and mind to work together in harmony. One is not better than the other. The shift allows the intuitive wisdom of your heart to lead instead of the power of your intellectual mind. You want your heart to be the first responder.

Self-Compassion

Self-compassion is a nonnegotiable responsibility of all earth angels. Self-compassion does not come naturally because we live in a world that's full of fear. Self-compassion is remembering your magnificence and unlearning judgment.

Self-compassion is a sign of spiritual maturity and is a quality you may spend lifetimes cultivating. When you express self-compassion, you set up an energetic blueprint that magnetizes that vibration to you. Practicing self-compassion every day allows you to carry more angelic love in your physical body and energy body. Self-compassion needs to be daily and intentional to increase your ability to receive more love from your angels.

Self-compassion is *not*:

- Indulging in self-pity
- Passive
- For the weak (it requires no effort, devotion, or creativity to judge yourself)
- Self-enabling (unhealthy behaviors)
- Hiding from yourself
- Victim mentality

Self-compassion:

- Accelerates spiritual growth
- Expands your earth angel medicine
- Heals your body and the planet
- Is an active practice
- Is fully seeing yourself

- Is vulnerable and tender
- Is magnetic
- Is liberating

When you commit to the practice of self-compassion, your parts know that you have their back. Your parts are not afraid that you will berate, dismiss, belittle, or exile them. Your parts need self-compassion to heal. Self-compassion is about fully seeing yourself. The path of the earth angel is to meet your vulnerabilities, your pain, and issues with self-compassion.

Self-compassion strengthens the muscle that allows you to see all of your parts. It's easy to love the parts of you that are happy, joyful, and that you are proud of. Having compassion for your parts that hate, judge, criticize, or get angry is what builds spiritual maturity. Fully seeing yourself—the light and the shadow—helps others do the same. Self-compassion will raise your personal vibration and the vibration of the planet. When you can feed yourself the sweetness of self-compassion, you become your most powerful self!

Chapter Twenty-four

Steps for Practice Three: Release and Lead With Your Heart

There are five steps for Practice Three: Release and Lead With Your Heart. Each step is designed to build on the previous step, as follows:

Step 1: Intention and Invitation
Step 2: Open Your Grateful Heart
Step 3: Relax Your Mind
Step 4: Release Hurt and Pain
Step 5: Receive Unconditional Love and Compassion

Step 1: Choose Your Intention and Invite the Archangels of Release and Lead With Your Heart

Remember, energy follows intention. Choose how you want to feel so the angels of your intention surround you. Your intention, or fuel, becomes the anchor for you to receive angelic pain relief. In this step, you will:

- Choose your intention
- Recite Archangel Invitation
- Pause, breathe, and receive
- Express gratitude

The Archangel Invitation I created is designed to welcome the medicine of the archangels of Release and Lead With Your Heart: Archangel Chamuel, Archangel Zadkiel, Archangel Azrael, and

Archangel Jeremiel. Each of these archangels carry a specific medicine, as follows:

Archangel Chamuel—Angel of Peace

- Unconditional love and peace
- Self-love and self-compassion
- Finding lost items

Archangel Zadkiel—Angel of Compassion

- Spiritual professor, violet flame and transformation
- Access akashic records and soul's blueprint
- Clairaudience

Archangel Azrael—Angel of Comfort

- Supports souls in transitioning
- Grief counselor
- Access angelic wisdom

Archangel Jeremiel—Angel of Mercy

- Forgiveness and mercy
- Loving life review
- *All is well* mindset

In order for the archangels to enter your aura and offer pain relief, you need to ask for and invite their help. You can use any number of prayers to invite the archangels' loving support. The invitation below is designed to welcome the medicine of the archangels of Release and Lead With Your Heart. Feel free to change or modify the invitation.

I invite the loving power of Archangel Chamuel, Archangel Zadkiel, Archangel Azrael, and Archangel Jeremiel to surround me and help me lead with my heart. I'm willing to release all the pain, hurt, heartache, and any blocks in my body and heart so I can receive more love and compassion from my angels. I ask that the healing I receive today be shared with all my relations in all directions of time.

After you recite the invitation, take three deep breaths. Pause and let yourself receive the archangels' loving presence into your body and any points of pain. It's common when you are first inviting the archangels into your space to feel some uncertainty, self-doubt, or skepticism about receiving pain relief from the angels. Be gentle and patient with the process. Humans say practice makes perfect; the angels say practice makes better.

Step 2: Open Your Grateful Heart

As an earth angel, you already have an open heart. Your angels are guiding you to your next level of heart opening. Your angels remind you that this step is nonnegotiable in order to release. In this step, you will:

- Invite Archangel Chamuel
- Focus on the feeling of gratitude
- Receive self-appreciation

We start with inviting Archangel Chamuel:

> *Thank you, Archangel Chamuel, for bringing the medicine of peace, compassion, and unconditional love to me and into my heart. I invite the pink healing light of Archangel Chamuel to open my heart to self-love and being an instrument of peace. Thank you for reminding me that I am the beloved one so I can love my pain and all of my parts unconditionally. I allow the angels of peace, compassion, and unconditional love to open my heart wider to assist the releasing process.*

The energy of gratitude opens your heart. Invite the angels of gratitude to help you focus on the feeling or a memory of gratitude, something that fills your heart with joy and appreciation. Allow this gratitude to gently expand your heart's capacity to be open and tender. You are safe to be open, tender, and vulnerable. This tenderness allows the angels access to your pain.

Opening your grateful heart allows you to appreciate all of who you are—the pain and the peace. Appreciating your whole self releases resistance and invites acceptance. Acceptance softens your heart and invites angelic pain relief.

Receiving self-appreciation looks like:

- Slowing down and appreciating your inner goodness
- Being grateful for your pain
- Being kind to your body and heart

Step 3: Relax Your Mind

The power of your breath is the main tool to slow your busy mind. You are not trying to stop your thinking; you are simply trying to slow your thoughts so you can welcome the loving thoughts of your angels. The goal is not *no thought*, the goal is space between your thoughts. This space between your thoughts is where creativity, divine solutions, miracles, and your intuition can be accessed, which supports the releasing process. In this step, you will:

- Invite Archangel Zadkiel
- Breathe to slow your thoughts
- Sync your heart and mind
- Choose angel thoughts

We start by inviting Archangel Zadkiel:

Thank you, Archangel Zadkiel, for bringing the medicine of compassion and transformation to me and into my heart and mind to slow down my thoughts. I invite the violet light of Archangel Zadkiel to quiet my mind and open my compassionate heart space. I allow the angels of compassion and transformation to sync my heart and mind and assist the releasing process.

Equalizing your inhalations and exhalations is a simple and effective way to slow your thoughts and create space for your angels' love to flow in. A mind-calming breath exercise is to count your inhalations and count your exhalations in equal measure. Inhale to the count of four and exhale to the count of four. Repeat this three to five times until you feel your busy mind quiet down. You can also suspend your breath for one count in between the inhalation and exhalation. Do not tighten your shoulders and abdomen muscles when you suspend your breath.

To sync your heart and mind, place your hands over your heart. Then take a deep breath in and out. Allow your relaxed mind to touch into your heart and rest there. You can also visualize Archangel Zadkiel placing one hand on your head and one hand gently on your heart to assist this process. Say silently or out loud, "I am ready to release pain and lead with my heart."

You can also sync your heart and mind by visualizing the infinity symbol flowing from the center of your brain and third eye, across your throat, and into your heart.

If the angels are thoughts of God, then aligning your mind with Divine mind will open your mind to angel thoughts. Angel thoughts are loving thoughts that come directly from God's mind and have the power to relax your mind and heal pain. Angel thoughts awaken the higher brain function that supports your body's ability to heal.

Aligning your mind with the highest vibrational angel thought will both relax your mind and open your heart. With a calm heart and mind, your ability to release pain is amplified. Simply say, "Thank you, angels, for aligning my mind with Divine mind." Then take a cleansing breath in and out, and let the angels do the work.

Step 4: Release Hurt and Pain

The releasing process is necessary to be able to receive more love from your angels; however, it is often a step your parts want to skip. It's totally normal for your parts to resist releasing for fear of feeling the pain or trauma over again. Your angels know it takes great courage to feel the buried pain. Archangel Azrael's wisdom and comfort will anchor in each safety net so you will not be overwhelmed when you release, even if the release feels intense at times. In this step, you will:

- Invite Archangel Azrael
- Welcome the safety nets
- Invite the lesson of the pain
- Release through body movement and emotions

We begin by inviting Archangel Azrael:

Thank you, Archangel Azrael, for bringing me the medicine of comfort and wisdom. I invite the soothing yellow light of Archangel Azrael to calm and comfort my body and heart so I can safely honor and release the pain. I allow the angels of comfort and wisdom to infuse the point of pain and my heart with their love to assist the gentle releasing process.

With the angels of comfort and wisdom and Archangel Azrael's help, you can now welcome the "safety nets." It's important to remember that the safety nets are there whether you directly ask for them or not. Of course if you consciously ask for them, they will increase in power and strength and help you move through the process:

As a reminder, the three safety nets are:

- Cushions of comfort
  - Extra bubble of comfort and compassion to support your release
  - Never flooded or feel full intensity of pain when you stay open to angels' love
- Release only when ready
  - Angels know what you are ready to release
  - Angels know to what degree you can release safely
  - If you are guided to release, you are ready!
- No rushing
  - No urgency from angels, only your ego parts
  - Trust divine order
  - Take your time releasing

An essential part of releasing is allowing yourself to be open to the lesson and blessing from the pain. Once you learn and integrate the lesson for the pain, you can release the pain and not have to repeat the same pattern. Simply ask, *"How is it that I have learned the lesson from this pain?"* Keep asking this question as you physically and emotionally release.

Remember, releasing happens in layers, and it's totally normal for your body to twitch, shudder, or move involuntarily. You can also help your body release by moving deliberately through practices such as: yoga, Tai Chi, Qi Gong, cardio, or dance, to name a few.

Releasing suppressed pain can often evoke an emotional response. Whether you feel like laughing, crying, or screaming, all emotional responses are welcomed by your angels. An emotional response can be a confirmation of release. Of course, there are some people who experience *healing without feeling* and have few to no emotions or body movement, and that's fine too. It's important to stay relaxed and trust your body's truthful wisdom.

Releasing is a vulnerable process that is not for the faint of heart. It takes great courage to feel your pain even just a little and open your tender heart once again. The more angelic love you receive, the more gentle the release will be.

Step 5: Receive Unconditional Love and Compassion

Receiving means allowing your angels' love to flow into the point of pain. You may receive through your breath. You may receive through your roots. You may receive through your inner vision or directly into your heart. However you receive, it's essential to take your time receiving after you have released the pain. In this step, you will:

- Invite Archangel Jeremiel
- Allow your angels' love into your heart and body
- Breathe and receive

You can begin by inviting Archangel Jeremiel:

Thank you, Archangel Jeremiel, for bringing me the medicine of mercy, compassion, and forgiveness. I invite the deep purple light of Archangel Jeremiel's mercy to increase my capacity for receiving angelic pain relief. I allow the angels of mercy, compassion, and forgiveness to fill my body and heart, softening my resistance to receiving. I now accept that all is well.

The angels know the depth of the pain you experienced. They know exactly how many lifetimes you may have repeated that same pattern. When you willingly let the pain go, there is a tender spot, like a scrape, where the releasing happened. After you release pain, fear, trauma, or any issue in the tissue, there is a healing and integration period where you will feel tender.

The angels liken this releasing and receiving process to falling and scraping your knee. The falling on your knee is the releasing. The knee scrape is the wound of pain that now needs attention. The receiving is a loving hand placing a healing balm or ointment on the open wound. The wound is tender to the touch but needs the ointment to completely heal.

Receiving is a gift of healing you give yourself to soothe the "open wound" where the pain once resided. Receiving love from your angels after a release seals the healing process like placing ointment and a bandage on a scraped knee. Receiving usually feels very good, calming, and stabilizing after any physical or emotional release.

Receiving your angels' compassion after a deep release is like drinking a big glass of water after running three miles. It's refreshing to receive and can make any level of release that just happened seem manageable.

It is necessary to receive after you release because you want to make sure that you seal the wound with love and compassion.

Conversely, you may find that you are receiving more before you release. This is totally normal. Actually, releasing and receiving often happen simultaneously. You are releasing because you are being filled with your angels' love and compassion, and you are receiving your angels' love so you can release more pain. Remember, Spirit is infinite and can work on multiple levels at the same time for your highest good and highest healing.

Chapter Twenty-five

Release and Lead With Your Heart: Guided Angel Meditation

Each practice has its own guided angel meditation to support and reinforce the practice itself as well as your connection to your angels. By using these guided angel meditations, you open yourself to receiving more of your angels' love to heal your pain.

Begin with your breath. Inhale deeply and exhale completely, relaxing your shoulders as you exhale. Thank your body for serving you so well and feel your soul inside your body. As you breathe, feel the vastness and love of your soul expand outside of your body, into your aura, and up toward your angels. Feel your loving angels welcoming all of your parts.

As you breathe, invite all of your angels, guardian angels, allies, beloved ancestors, and the archangels of Release and Lead With Your Heart: Archangel Chamuel, angel of peace; Archangel Zadkiel, angel of compassion; Archangel Azrael, the angel of comfort; and Archangel Jeremiel, angel of mercy. Welcome the light of God, Source, Creator, and all the healing angels to be here now. Say, "Thank you for guiding and protecting me with your healing light for my highest good and highest healing. I am the keeper of my mind and body, and I welcome only those angels and guides that love me unconditionally."

Renew your devotion. Gently place your hands over your heart, the gateway of angels' love, and say silently, "I am devoted to receiving self-compassion from my angels." Open your heart to your angels' love. "I am devoted to receiving self-compassion from my angels." Align your mind with Divine mind. "I am devoted to receiving self-compassion from my angels." Receive your angels' devotion for you.

Relax and cherish your body. Welcome physical relaxation as you soften and relax your muscles from your bones and let go of tension from your back, neck, and shoulders. Visualize roots of light flowing through your legs and feet deep into the heart of Mother Earth. Feel Mother Earth receiving you. Trust the wisdom of your roots to connect with the perfect crystals, trees, and ancestor medicine for you today, strengthening your ability to release more and receive more.

As you breathe, welcome emotional relaxation as you trust that all of you is seen, heard, held, and loved. Feel your guardian angels acknowledging all of your feelings and all of your parts, allowing your emotions to calm and your body to relax even more.

Welcome mental relaxation as you allow your mind to slow down and gently focus on your breath. Follow the length of your breath to the top of your inhalation. Then follow the length of your breath to the bottom of your exhalation. Allow the space between your thoughts where all miracles, creativity, and your intuition reside to open and balance each chakra with the medicine of compassion.

As you breathe, welcome spiritual relaxation as you surrender into the arms of your angels and expand your auric field. Trust the benevolent divine plan unfolding for your highest good and for all those you love.

Release and lead with your heart. As you breathe, welcome Archangel Chamuel to open the front of your heart and the back of your heart with deep gratitude. Allow this gratitude to fill your heart to overflowing with joy and appreciation. Feel Archangel Chamuel radiate the peace that surpasses understanding deep into the chambers of your heart, releasing hurt, betrayal, pain, and any blocks to self-compassion. Receive Archangel Chamuel's mantra, "I am the beloved one," into your heart and mind as you welcome peace, peace, and perfect peace.

As you breathe, welcome Archangel Zadkiel's deep compassion into your heart, body, mind, and soul. Feel Archangel Zadkiel's unconditional compassion release and dissolve all harshness, self-judgment, and disappointment from all of your parts and deep into the nucleus of your cells. Visualize Archangel Zadkiel's violet flame of transformation in front of you. Receive the violet flame into your heart to transform and release inner harshness and increase your self-compassion quotient.

As you breathe, welcome Archangel Jeremiel and the legions of angels of mercy to surround your heart and your aura. Feel the tenderness, mercy, and forgiveness of Archangel Jeremiel's love release the layers of trauma from past difficulties, self-abuse, and any grievances from your body and heart. Welcome this merciful compassion for yourself and your soul's journey as you see yourself through the eyes of your guardian angels. Feel Archangel Jeremiel bless each layer of your aura with the vibration of All is Well. Your physical, emotional, mental, spiritual, and karmic layers of your aura are blessed and vibrating, and All is Well.

As you breathe, welcome Archangel Azrael to comfort your beautiful heart. Feel Archangel Azrael soothing and calming your grieving, sad, and lonely parts. Feel the wise counsel of your soul and your guardian angels fill your heart with deep compassion, comfort, and calm so you can be an instrument of peace. As an instrument of peace, you can open your heart wider to the wise and compassionate counsel of your beloved ancestors and angels. You are safe and spiritually protected in all ways.

Trust that releasing happens in layers, and it's totally normal for your body to twitch or shudder and for your emotions to rise and fall as you release. Support your release by asking your angels, "How is it that I have learned the lesson from this pain?" Take all the time that you need in this releasing process as you let go of what no longer serves you. Allow your angels to bring your heart and mind into unison. With your heart and mind in sync, you are safe to release and lead with your heart. You are safe to release, release, release.

Receive and trust your intuition. As you breathe, relax your body and mind even deeper and let yourself receive all the love, healing, and gentleness you need. Trust that your angels are always communicating with you through your psychic senses. Welcome the angels of intuition to bless each intuitive channel with compassion.

You are safe to trust what you see, feel, hear, know, sense, and smell in the sacred moment in time. Allow yourself to receive all of the love, compassion, and forgiveness that you need to heal your pain. You are safe to receive, receive, receive.

Receive a final blessing of compassion and unconditional love from the archangels of Release and Lead With Your Heart and your own guardian angels. Say, "I ask that all the healing I receive today be shared with all my relations in all directions of time."

Take a cleansing breath in and out. Gently bow to your angels as you bring your hands to prayer mudra (position) and feel them bow to you with gratitude, devotion, and deep compassion, sealing your meditation with a Namaste (or an Amen, or other word you prefer).

PRACTICE FOUR

Receive and Trust Your Intuition

Chapter Twenty-six

From Trauma Into Trust

Trauma can block you from trusting your intuition. The story I am telling today is still very tender, and in truth, I am still learning and alchemizing from the experience. What I have learned is that when you share your story, you transform the pain into peace and the trauma into spiritual understanding.

I woke up in mid-November three years ago with excruciating pain in my left hip. It was my second day teaching basic IET training at Infinity Foundation. IET stands for Integrated Energy Therapy, a form of healing with the angels that uses the angelic energy of compassion to transform pain into peace. I was so excited and honored to share my medicine at this well-known spiritual center. Teaching IET at Infinity was a milestone in my evolving career as an Angel Professional.

I used a PowerPoint as part of the training and asked to borrow my mom's laptop. She dropped it off that Sunday morning before her shift at the hospital. She was shaking like a leaf. I asked her what was wrong, and she said my brother had been missing for two days. My parts felt surprised and even a little angry that she hadn't told me my brother was missing.

When I found out the news that Dylan was missing, I immediately tapped into my intuition to see if I could locate him. I assumed he was with an old friend and reached out to her. She got back right away and said that he was not with her. I could sense her worry and concern over the text message.

I went to Infinity to teach the second part of my IET training. It was a peaceful and healing day. I was so grateful to be doing my life's purpose and training people to channel angel love into their bodies. As the day progressed, though, I could feel my anxiety rising as I wondered where my brother could be.

On the way home from the training, I got a strong intuitive idea of who my brother was with before he went missing. I clearly heard a name in my mind. Sure enough, my intuition was correct and Dylan was with the person the angels had named the night of his traumatic car accident.

At 4 PM that Sunday, my mom called me crying. She said that the police were at her house, and that Dylan had been in a serious car accident. Filled with dread at the news of this accident, my husband, my mom, and I jumped in the van to drive downtown.

The drive to the hospital was horrendous that day. There was heavy traffic and my anxiety was increasing with each mile. My mom's parts were scared, and I just remembered praying really hard. I was sending Archangel Michael, Archangel Raphael, Mother Mary, and all the healing angels to him before we knew any details or the extent of his injuries. I had a horrible feeling in the pit of my stomach.

The first sight of Dylan laying in the hospital bed all swollen and intubated contributed to my PTSD. I can still hear the sounds of the beeping machines and the ventilator as well as the rush of the ICU nurses tending to all of his life-threatening issues and injuries. When I could speak, I immediately wanted to know the exact injuries he experienced.

The nurse began to read off his list of injuries, which included: an open book pelvic fracture, a compound fracture of his left femur, a fracture of the tibial plateau, a fracture of the fibula, a lacerated liver, a collapsed left lung, and worst of all, a traumatic brain injury (or TBI). While hearing his list of injuries, my knees gave out, and I crumbled to the ground.

As a sensitive soul, my first concern was how much pain he was in. My first and only surgery was my ACL replacement. I could not even imagine the pain of several surgeries in a few days' time to repair all of his broken bones and damaged organs. In that stressful and terrifying moment, we had no idea we'd be in the ICU for four more weeks while my brother fought to stay alive.

There were so many synchronicities in this traumatic event that made me slow down and pay attention to the angels' guidance. One that stood out immediately was that all of Dylan's broken bones were on his left side, where the feminine energy resides. I'd woken up that morning with my left hip throbbing in pain. I wondered if I was transmuting some of his pain through my own left hip.

There were numerous life-threatening complications in my brother's recovery that made his four weeks in the intensive care unit heart-wrenching and deeply stressful. Dylan had rhabdomyolysis (rhabdo), meaning his kidneys were shutting down due to the immense trauma to his bones, organs, and muscle tissues. He had a total of seven major surgeries in six weeks' time, with six of them during the first week after the accident.

The mixture of terror, grief, and stress was enough to crush anyone. I think what was different about this trauma was that I was walking through it awake. I knew that I had to keep my intuition open to my angels' guidance, and I didn't want to suppress my feelings about the experience.

The only thing that kept me going was my spiritual practice. My faith deepened as I used all of my spiritual tools and energy work, alongside the power of prayer, to help Dylan fight for his life. I set up an altar with crystals, sacred objects, and angel oracle cards on the window ledge of his ICU hospital room. When you looked at his swollen and broken body, it was easy to dip into fear and worry. Having the altar and the oracle cards there in the room helped me to raise my vibration so I could stay connected to my angels.

The angel oracle cards calmed my mind, helping me stay focused on the divine guidance from the angels instead of listening to my worried and fearful parts. The oracle cards also opened up my intuitive channels so that I could hear what Dylan's body needed in each moment. Of course, there was immense surrender because the ICU nurses and doctors were in charge. The highest truth, though, was that God was in charge.

The ICU was so intense that it was easy to let my parts slip into fear and play out worst-case scenarios. The angels led me to the Mul mantra, a healing mantra that I chanted multiple times throughout the day to calm my mind and help me receive love from my angels. I would play the mantra when I was at the hospital and chant it while sitting with my brother.

Dylan had so many injuries that it was hard to fathom how he survived the accident. The open book pelvic fracture (when the pelvis breaks open like a book) severed many major nerves and arteries and is typically a fatal injury. The doctors believed he survived because he was young and in excellent physical shape. Dylan was an American Ninja Warrior.

I thank God and the angels for the many synchronicities that kept my intuition open and my faith strong when my parts were crumbling under the stress, grief, and fear of this traumatic experience. The first week at the ICU was mostly a blur, but one synchronicity filled me with hope, and I remember it clearly.

One of my brother's friends, a resident at the hospital, was doing rounds and came to visit Dylan after hearing of his accident. Dylan's friend said he was normally never at this hospital doing rounds, but happened to be there that day. Although I was at the hospital a lot, I wasn't usually there during the day, so running into my brother's friend felt significant to me.

He looked me in the eyes and said that no one should have survived this accident based on the list of intense injuries. Dylan's friend said he was immensely lucky to be alive, and it was because he was in such good shape. I felt like this chance meeting was a message of hope while Dylan laid in a coma fighting for his life.

Dylan's list of injuries was extensive, and my angels had me focus the healing on his kidneys. His kidneys were failing, and he needed to be on continuous dialysis. Alongside prayer, the most effective energy medicine tool I used was the angelic energy of safety from the IET system I had just been teaching.

I was grateful my angels led me to focus on healing his kidneys even though the doctors were giving up hope. Earth angels everywhere were supporting me during this traumatic and stressful time. We used essential oils, crystals, energy work, and prayer to restore Dylan's kidney health.

My stress levels were extremely high during the four weeks he was in the ICU, and I was beginning to show symptoms of PTSD.

I am so grateful that my devotion to the angels and my spiritual practice kept me grounded and present despite the tremendous pain and stress.

Being in the midst of the aftermath of this car accident was like being on a terrifying roller coaster. The long list of life-threatening complications was only worsened when my brother coded. I'll never forget the sequence of events on the Monday after his accident that, despite all odds, strengthened my faith in God and the angels.

I picked up my mom that Monday to head down to the hospital again. It had only been eight days since we found out about the accident, but it felt like a lifetime. We were both completely exhausted. To make matters more distressing, on the way downstairs, my mom tripped and fell, horribly twisting her left ankle. She was in a lot of pain when she got into the van. My mom's ankle was immediately swollen and bruised. Her left foot and ankle up to her calf were black and blue.

There was that left side connection synchronicity again. My mom twisting and bruising her left ankle felt very connected with the emotional pain that she was experiencing from Dylan's accident. I also wondered if she was energetically transmuting some of his left side pain as well.

My mom was losing her faith. Although I don't believe in being negative, I can understand why my mom's parts felt hopeless. The endless complications that kept our cortisol levels through the roof and the fear of my brother being in a vegetative state triggered a deep despair in my mom.

As we were sitting in the hospital room while they were hooking Dylan up to the dialysis machine, hopelessness was taking over my mom, and she kept repeating the negative thought, "This is so horrible," over and over again. For just a minute, I started to get sucked into the negativity and once or twice agreed with her and said, "Yes, this is so horrible."

It was like a movie. Within a minute of this negative thought, Dylan coded and immediately turned blue. The ICU nurses and doctors rushed in and ushered us out to the waiting room. I remember thinking, *"Is this it? Is he going to die?"*

Seeing my brother turn blue and code was another unforgettable PTSD memory. I dropped to my knees in the corner of the waiting room and prayed hard. Through a flood of tears, I repeated Hail Mary over and over. I immediately texted two friends who have powerful prayers.

While deep in prayer for God to save my brother, time stopped. Finally, the ICU doctor came out and told us that he was stable. Dylan experienced a pulmonary embolism as the dialysis machine sucked a blood clot from his lower leg into his lungs. That may have been one of the most terrifying moments of my life.

After witnessing the power of a negative thought in slow motion, I needed to strengthen my devotion to receiving from my angels and to trust the power of prayer. I focused on gratitude. I was deeply grateful that Dylan was in one of the best hospitals in the country with top doctors and nurses at his side.

After four horrendous weeks and many other complications, Dylan finally moved from the ICU into the medical unit for another six weeks. The pace between the units was eye-opening. The ICU was an intense, fast-paced unit with an instant response to any request. The medical unit worked with a much slower response to issues, and it took time to get used to the different pace. Of course, I am deeply grateful for the medical interventions and medications that saved my brother's life.

Dylan and my mom spent Christmas in the medical unit that year. During his stay there, the two main concerns were the severity of his TBI and his kidney function. There are many layers to his TBI and how Dylan bounced back. Our main focus was getting Dylan the brain support he needed. His best hope for healing from the traumatic brain injury was to get into the well-known rehabilitation facility across from the hospital. However, they would not admit him to the brain rehab facility while he still required four days of dialysis.

Healing my brother's kidneys became my main mission so he could be accepted into the brain rehab facility, otherwise he would go to a nursing home. The prognosis was looking grim. The chief nephrologist reported that his kidneys appeared to be in end-stage renal failure, and he would need dialysis for the rest of his life.

I knew deep in my heart that this would not be his fate. I kept praying, using mantra, angel oracle cards, crystals, and an awesome blend of essential oils on Dylan almost everyday. If I wasn't there in person, I would do the energy work from a distance.

Miraculously, by the grace of God, almost overnight, Dylan went from end-stage renal failure and four days of dialysis to his kidneys coming back on line and fully functioning on their own. It was beyond a New Year's miracle. Thank you, angels.

The kidney miracle led to another, as Dylan was able to go straight from the medical unit at the hospital to the brain rehab facility, where he spent five or six weeks. It was a blessing to see Dylan talk and walk again. Although he had a very long recovery ahead, and there were still many uncertainties, things were looking up.

Upon being released from the brain rehab facility to go home, Dylan went from a wheelchair, to a walker, to a cane, to walking without any support, to riding his bike within just a few short months. He had two more major bone graft surgeries for his left femur, making a total of nine surgeries from his accident. Finally, although his physical body was healing, mentally and emotionally there was a long way to go. Healing from a traumatic brain injury is difficult. Dylan has a right brain injury, which means that his intuitive and social filters are strongly challenged—he basically has no filter—making for a very tricky recovery.

In retrospect, walking consciously through this trauma strengthened my faith and my earth angel medicine. I had to lean into my intuition and my healing abilities to remain open to my angels' loving guidance. This traumatic experience reignited my PTSD and blocked my intuition at times because the fear and worry were so intense. As a result, the trauma required me to slow down and go within for answers. It challenged me to trust God's plan and the divine order despite outward appearances. The greater the fear I felt, the more faith I had to summon so I could stay in the flow of receiving from my angels. The trauma of Dylan's situation led to a level of trust I had not previously experienced.

Chapter Twenty-seven

What is Receiving?

Receiving is the ability to allow, accept, and assimilate through your senses the angel medicine and messages in each moment. The angels are always guiding you to receive more. Conscious receiving is an act of self-love that magnetizes angelic pain relief. Your angels understand that you may have fears around receiving. You may fear that if you are open to receiving, you will receive bad or negative experiences. The fear of receiving something we don't want or receiving "bad" energy or information can cause you to limit or filter your receiving channels. This is a false perception. Receiving—especially after releasing—is just the next step in healing your body and reclaiming your magnificence.

Receiving allows you to give from a place of peace so you do not become depleted. Many earth angels are really good at giving and being of service but can have a difficult time receiving. Your parts may worry that it's selfish or unfair for you to receive. Of course, your angels know the only way to truly give is to receive and trust the unconditional love of God and the angels. Conscious receiving is nonnegotiable to healing your pain with angelic love.

Receiving is *not*:

- Selfish
- Being overloaded with too much information or energy

- Absorbing other people's pain or worries
- Carrying the burdens of others
- Rescuing, fixing, or controlling others

Receiving is:

- A courageous and conscious practice
- Being tender and gentle
- Accepting your power and peace
- Allowing access and passage of angel energy and information into your body
- Assimilating through your senses from a place of peace and empowerment

Receiving requires courage because in order to heal the pain in your body, you have to allow that pain to surface. You are guided to trust that the pain is a portal to receiving angelic love. Receiving is a vulnerable and necessary practice to experience angelic pain relief.

There are several ways to consciously receive from your angels. Each practice in this book builds and strengthens the foundation of receiving love from your angels. Ways to receive include:

- Intention
- Breath
- Relaxation
- Releasing
- Energy body and physical body
- Intuition

Intention. Remember, energy follows intention. If your intention is to receive angelic pain relief, then you will. Simply set your intention to receive and let the angels do the work.

Breath. You are receiving oxygen with every inhalation and releasing carbon dioxide with every exhalation. As you have read throughout this book, your breath is a powerful healing tool. Your breath helps you relax your body and mind. Your breath helps you release tension and pain. Your breath can guide you back to your body and the present moment. Your breath is also a tool to increase your capacity to receive loving pain relief from your angels.

Relaxation. As you know, relaxation is the gateway to angelic pain relief. Relaxing your body and mind creates space in your physical and energetic body to receive the healing pain relief you need. When your body is tight or tense, there is not as much space to receive. Moving consciously through the four levels of relaxation creates space to take in and receive your angels' unconditional love.

Releasing. Releasing and receiving are as natural as breathing. However, releasing may take some effort if your pain has been suppressed for some time. Releasing pain creates space to receive angelic love, and receiving angelic love helps you release pain. Although these are two distinct practices and steps, they often happen simultaneously. This is because Source love is infinite and all-encompassing.

Energy Body. You are always breathing; therefore, you are always receiving. As an earth angel, you are guided to tend to your energy body through the practices in this book to increase your ability and capacity to receive healing pain relief from your angels. Your energy body is designed to receive angelic pain relief. Your roots, parts, chakras, and aura are each designed to assimilate and receive divine love in all its forms. You were born to receive healing pain relief from your angels.

Once your energy body receives the pain relief, it naturally integrates into your physical body. This can happen without your conscious awareness of it, like how breathing is controlled by the autonomic nervous system. Of course, as you become conscious of this subtle energy, your ability to receive expands.

Intuition. Your intuition is a strong and clear source of receiving angelic pain-relieving messages. Your five direct clair channels are attuned to receiving angelic pain relief through your focused intention. You always have the free will choice to follow your intuition or not.

Observe all the ways in which the Creator invites you to receive unconditional love and compassion from the angelic realm. Once you get comfortable receiving more love from your angels, you are guided to trust your intuition and take action on that guidance. Ask and you shall receive.

Chapter Twenty-eight

What Is Intuition?

Intuition is defined as the ability to understand something immediately without the need for conscious reasoning. Intuition may also be described as a hunch, feeling, instinct, inkling, or premonition. Your intuition is your inner GPS. This inner guidance system is the direct way in which your angels communicate with you. There are two types of intuition highlighted in this book: direct and indirect angel guidance.

Intuition is like a direct telephone line to the Divine, and the phone number is in your heart stored under *gratitude*. When you align your intuition with your angels' love, you will increase the bandwidth of your intuitive guidance. There are five direct intuitive channels, also known as clair channels, like radio stations where you can receive divine guidance.

Everyone is born with intuition. You could say it's hardwired in. Earth angels are highly intuitive souls who can sense energy beyond normal human limits.

It's important to note that everyone has all five intuitive clair channels. We are all equal in God's eyes, and no one was given more intuitive abilities than another. However, because of the law of free will, you can choose to use these gifts or deny that they exist, even if they're in your blueprint. The choice is always yours.

God is very wise and infinitely loving. The Creator would not leave you without multiple channels of connection. God knows the courage it takes your soul to be human and embody.

Source gave you direct access to all the energy, information, and pain-relieving messages you need to live out your earth angel mission. As an earth angel, you are here to awaken your intuition and be a light in this world. Your happiness and pain relief is your angels' top priority.

Typically, you will have one clair channel that is most open, clear, and comfortable. Part of your evolution as an earth angel is to awaken and develop all five intuitive channels in balance so that you stay open to receiving all of the love, healing, and messages your angels have for you. Although pain is a portal, it can also slow the flow of receiving intuitive angel messages.

When you rely on only your strongest intuitive channel, you may miss out on deeper or more complete pain-relieving messages from the angels. Developing your five clairs in balance and trusting your intuition is a lifelong practice. Trusting your intuition expands your earth angel medicine, heals pain in your body, and empowers your soul's journey.

Remember, God and the angels love you unconditionally and want you to hear, see, feel, know, and trust their messages. Your angels' messages are not secret or even that mysterious. They are, however, sacred and valuable information for your ascension as an earth angel. Healing the pain and other issues in the tissues from your body is part of your earth angel mission.

You have the ability to clearly connect with your team of angels through your intuition. The benevolent, loving Source energy would never deny you access to its unconditional love, especially for the sacred work of healing your physical body.

Trusting Your Intuition

Trust is defined as a firm belief in the reliability, truth, ability, and strength in someone or something. Trust takes spiritual maturity and courage to allow your angels and the Divine to lead the way. Your angels are always guiding you toward self-trust and reminding you that you are one with the Divine.

You are safe in this lifetime to trust yourself and your angels' divine guidance. It is common for earth angels to experience self-doubt and distrust if you were ever hurt, shamed, or judged after trusting and following your intuition. Your intuition is a reliable source of energy and information. Trusting your intuition builds the strength and reliability of your angelic connection.

Trusting your senses is a skill you develop, like building muscles. If you want to build your tricep muscle, you need to lift free weights many times to grow stronger. It is the same with building trust; you must practice receiving messages and relying on your inner truth over and over again to develop that skill. Trust is a muscle to develop, like your triceps.

Trust is like faith's sibling. Faith is defined as complete confidence in someone or something. As an earth angel, your ability to receive love and healing requires confidence in the benevolence and compassion of Source love. Faith is knowing in your heart you are loved unconditionally. Building trust requires you to have faith in your inherent goodness and wholeness, no matter how intense your pain gets.

Trusting what you see, feel, hear, know, sense, and smell in each moment is a skill you can enhance and balance. Trust that your angels' messages and guidance are for your highest good and highest healing. Your angels know that trust can be difficult if you've experienced abuse, trauma, or pain. However, trust is an essential step to honoring your intuition as a way to receive love from your angels to heal your body.

Trust is closely linked to divine order. A big part of the earth angel mission is to trust divine order. Your angels guide you to be devoted to the belief that there is a benevolent divine plan unfolding for your highest good and for everyone you love.

Divine order means that everything in the universe is in perfect order and harmony in alignment with unconditional love. This is a difficult concept for the ego to grasp because when you look at the 3D world, there appears to be pain and suffering. Through your human eyes, this suffering appears real, yet the divine truth says that suffering is an illusion. Divine order beckons you to see through the illusion of suffering and to keep a steadfast focus on the love that is present. This takes great spiritual maturity and is not for the faint of heart.

Your angels will never hurt, scare or intentionally upset you. Your angels know exactly what you need to heal pain. The truth is, when you receive divine guidance through your "clairs" (see the next chapter), you are ready to receive it, and the messages will be for your highest good. This is what it means to trust in a benevolent and loving universe.

Awareness Expands Intuition

Awareness is the ability to directly know and perceive, to feel and be cognizant of events. Awareness is the state of being conscious of something. Awareness is truly the first step in awakening to your angels' loving presence. Your angels guide you to the awareness that you are already intuitive. You, like everyone, were born with all five intuitive channels. As an earth angel, awareness of your intuition expands your intuition.

Once you acknowledge that you are already intuitive, you can begin to expand your perception beyond just your five senses and into your psychic senses. As your perception expands, you can gather and receive energy and information that can bring you pain relief. *Your angels' guidance will always be trustworthy, supportive, and lead you toward healing pain relief.*

Consciousness is defined as the state of being fully alert, aware, oriented, and responsive to your environment. Your consciousness is ever-expanding through your focus and attention on it. When you affirm and allow your consciousness to grow in each moment, you open up to more levels of receiving angelic pain relief.

There are many levels of consciousness to experience as a human. Trusting your intuition is an act of self-compassion that expands your conscious awareness of your angels' love. Your expanded consciousness allows greater amounts of love and healing to enter your physical body to release pain. Awareness is a gift that awakens and expands your dormant intuitive abilities.

What Is Synchronicity?

Synchronicity is an experience of two or more events which occur in a meaningful manner, but which are causally unrelated. For example, my left hip was hurting badly the morning I found out my brother's left femur and pelvis were broken. Synchronicity is the language of the universe. It provides guide posts along the way to support you in trusting that God and the angels have your back. The more your consciousness opens to synchronicities, the more they will multiply.

When you are just beginning to tap into your intuition, instances of synchronicity can seem to be so subtle and far between that you may dismiss them. However, watching for and trusting the synchronicity your angels show you will validate your earth angel journey and calm your parts that are in pain. The more you pay attention to the signs and synchronicities your angels send, the more they will increase in frequency and potency.

Tenderness and Vulnerability

Tenderness is defined as a feeling of concern, gentle affection, and warmth. This is how your angels feel about you and your body. Your angels genuinely care for your well-being like a loving mother does for her child. On the path of the earth angel, it's important to let your defenses down and let in your angels' love through your intuitive channels.

Tenderness is a quality of your heart chakra that creates space for your angels' unconditional love to flow into your body. Being tender allows you to receive. You can practice tenderness by being gentle with yourself and your body. Being gentle with your body, mind, and parts is a lifelong practice, like self-compassion, and yields a bounty of clear and empowered intuitive gifts.

The focus on gentleness applies to your physical body and your energy body. Practicing being gentle with your body and energy body opens an increased flow of angelic messages and love that will release the pain or any issue in the tissue. *Gentleness increases your intuition. Gentleness helps you relax and trust your angels' love is true.*

Vulnerability may seem scary because it's often defined as being easily hurt or harmed. However, the angels know that vulnerability is not a weakness, it's a strength. Many earth angels shy away from vulnerability for fear of being judged or called weak. The fear of judgment for being vulnerable is very real and causes many sensitive souls to armor up. However, the more vulnerable you can be, the more access you have to deeper truths and healing intuitive guidance. Likewise, your vulnerability allows your angels access and passage into your energy body, which can provide angelic pain relief.

Being tender requires the strength to let go of your defenses and barriers to your angels' love. When the barriers to love are released, your humanity grows. Earth angels are meant to be human and make mistakes. The angels say that life is not about perfection, it's about presence. Your gentle and loving presence is a gift, not only to your body, but to all those you are here to serve.

The common fear of making a mistake when following your intuitive guidance can be paralyzing at times, especially if you have past life burdens. The fear of failure stops many earth angels from trusting their intuitive gifts and abilities. Fear of rejection, humiliation, persecution, and abandonment are common fears that shut down your intuitive gifts.

You are safe to fail, make mistakes, to forget, and to fall because the angels have your back. It requires both courage and gentleness to receive and trust the intuitive guidance your angels are sending. Your angels honor your courage to embody and be a divine being living a human experience.

Chapter Twenty-nine

Direct Angel Guidance

Direct angel guidance comes directly into your body through your physical senses as well as through your psychic senses. Your five psychic senses are your intuitive channels also known as the five "clairs." You are continuously receiving direct angel messages through your five intuitive channels, which are:

- Claircognizance — clear thought
- Clairvoyance — clear vision
- Clairaudience — clear hearing
- Clairfragrance — clear scent (can include clear taste, or clairgustance)
- Clairsentience — clear feeling

Each clair is an access point for your angels to send you love, which can heal physical pain. Your clair access points help you tend to both your physical body and energy body. Just like each layer of your energy body is connected with a physical elimination system, so are your psychic senses connected with your physical senses.

Each intuitive clair channel (except claircognizance) links to one of the physical senses of sight, hearing, smell/taste, and touch. As an earth angel, your physical senses are just as important as your psychic senses to stay in the flow of your angels' love.

Receiving from your angels through your intuitive channels requires devotion and discipline because there are many fears to overcome. These fears slow the flow of your angels' loving intuitive messages. Some common fears of opening all five intuitive channels include the fear of:

- Feeling unworthy or not good enough
- Being hurt or hurting others
- Rejection, persecution, and abandonment
- Seeing your shadow
- Seeing your whole self fully
- Past life trauma or pain
- Being overwhelmed
- Being judged or shamed
- Being stuck or drowning in the pain

Each of the five clairs are portals for your angels' love and messages to flow in and heal your pain. Whether it's physical or emotional pain, your angels are always communicating with you through your physical and psychic senses. Now, let's delve a little deeper and explore each of the five clairs.

Claircognizance

- Clear thought or clear knowing
- Crown chakra
- Psychic sense of thought or 6th sense
- Archangel Uriel and Archangel Jophiel

Claircognizance, which means clear knowing or clear thought, is connected with your crown chakra, brain, and nervous system. The crown chakra, also known as the thousand-petal lotus, is the receiver of your answered prayers into your physical body through your thoughts. Claircognizance is known as a metaphysical sense where you know something to be correct but may not be able to back up your statement with a fact or an explanation of how you came into that information.

Claircognizance is the one clair that is not directly connected with one of the five physical senses, but rather the psychic sense of thought, sometimes called the 6th sense. Claircognizance shows up as receiving angel messages through your thoughts. Claircognizance can range from the most basic knowing of how to operate a tool you have never used before to knowing ancient divine teachings that you never learned consciously in this life.

Claircognizant thoughts will create high vibrational feelings in your body and mind. When you experience a claircognizant thought, you feel uplifted, peaceful, empowered, and joyful, like all angel messages. This intuitive channel is often overlooked or dismissed because you have so many thoughts per day. It takes a discerning and very focused mind to recognize a divine thought through the barrage of the 70,000 thoughts you have each day. Claircognizance gives you the ability to hear the thoughts of God. When this happens, there's no judgment attached to the thought and/or you feel emotionally neutral, which is a way to be sure it is divinely inspired.

Another aspect of claircognizance is being able to "know" what someone else is thinking, or even to be able to read other people's thoughts. Knowing what someone else is thinking can only be accessed when you have reached a certain level of spiritual maturity and self-knowledge. You have to attain a high level of integrity and self-compassion to be able to access this level of claircognizance.

It's important to say here that all of your intuitive gifts need to be used in service of the light and for divine love. Your gifts are only meant to be used to heal. You never want to use your intuitive gifts to intentionally cause harm. Using your gifts against the highest good will create constrictive karma for you.

The shadow of claircognizance is:

- Playing mind games or twisting words
- Thinking you are better than someone
- Playing God by trying to control the outcome of a situation
- Overthinking or negative thinking
- Guilt
- Paranoia or dissociation

Clairvoyance

- Clear vision
- Third eye chakra
- Physical sense of sight
- Archangel Raziel, Archangel Raphael, and Mother Mary

Clairvoyance is defined as the power or faculty of discerning objects not present to the senses, or the ability to perceive matters beyond the range of ordinary perception. Clairvoyance literally translates to clear vision or clear sight and is connected with the third eye chakra. Clairvoyance shows up as a mental movie or images in your mind's eye that are the answer to your prayers and intentions.

Your inner vision is one of the many ways your angels communicate with you. Sometimes your clairvoyance is like a brain flash, where you see a quick vision or image of what you are asking about. For example, if you lose your keys and you ask, "Where are my keys?" You may see an image flash into your mind revealing their location on your bed or in your coat pocket.

As an earth angel, your clairvoyance is essential because it is the fastest way for your angels to give you messages. The old adage,

"A picture is worth a thousand words," describes why your clairvoyance is such an important clair channel in receiving instant angelic pain relief. Remember, your angels' messages will feel calm, neutral, and peaceful, never scary or stressful.

Clairvoyance is not about seeing the future, predicting events before they happen, or planning for worst case scenarios. Clairvoyance is about clearly seeing inside yourself. Clairvoyance is the ability to clearly see the love and light in each pain or issue. Your clairvoyance invites you to clearly see your parts, your light, and the angels' messages through your inner vision. Trust is the medicine that opens your clairvoyant third eye.

The center of clairvoyance is the third eye, also known as the "ajna" in the yogic tradition. Ajna in Sanskrit translates to: "perceive," "command," or "beyond wisdom." The third eye is located between your eyes at the brow and is connected with the pineal gland. Your third eye, when awakened, will often look like an actual eye. The seed sound for your third eye is OM, the sacred sound of the universe. Your angels remind you that you are safe in this lifetime to trust your clairvoyant inner vision.

It's essential as an earth angel to reclaim your clairvoyance. There are often past life burdens connected with your clairvoyance if you were a seer, a healer, a medicine woman, or a witch. Although everyone is born with all five clairs, you need to develop these abilities like building muscles. Often, people were frightened of those healers who seemed to possess extrasensory abilities. As a result, seers and healers were often demonized, persecuted, or killed for these natural gifts.

The shadow of clairvoyance is:

- Self-doubt, worry, and distrust
- Indecisiveness and confusion
- Fear of making a mistake

- Fear of seeing too much or seeing something scary
- Fear of seeing your own divinity
- Planning worst-case scenarios

Clairaudience

- Clear hearing
- Ear chakras
- Physical sense of hearing
- Archangel Orion, Archangel Zadkiel, and Archangel Michael

Clairaudience means clear hearing and is connected with the ear chakras and inner ear organs. Clairaudience is defined as the capability to receive intuitive vocal messages from the world of spirit. It's important to note that most clairaudient messages from your angels will be in your own voice. The angels will only use their voice or a more booming voice if you are not paying attention to the subtle messages, or if you are in grave danger. Simply knowing that the angels' messages will be in your own voice will open your clairaudient channel.

Clairaudience is a subtle channel and takes patience to cultivate. Your angels' messages will always be trustworthy, loving, peaceful, and bring you relief. Clairaudience is about hearing the voices of your angels and the voice of love. If any messages make you feel bad or unworthy, that is not your angels. Painful or scary messages can be from your parts or possibly an unsupportive outside energy.

When your clairaudience is open, you are also attuned to the whispers of your body. Your body will give you messages that help you stay in the flow of your angels' love. Your body will not betray you. If your body is in pain, it just needs more love.

Receiving clairaudient angel messages through this channel will increase your ability to hear and listen to the messages from your parts. Your inner dialogue is often your parts trying to get your attention. Your angels whisper and have soft and calming tones. Your parts may be loud, especially if they are in pain. Having an inner dialogue with your parts is totally normal and your clairaudience channel supports that conversation. Clairaudience can sometimes be downplayed for a fear of being judged for "hearing voices."

Clairaudience can also show up as hearing a high-pitched ringing in one or both ears for a few seconds. This type of ringing often precedes receiving an angelic download. When this high-pitched noise happens, it's important to pause and pay attention to each clair to discern the message. If the clairaudient message is unclear, ask for more clarity.

The shadow of clairaudience is:

- Listening to the voice of fear
- Being self-critical or hard on yourself
- Believing negative or painful messages
- Fear of hearing something you don't want to hear
- Fear of being judged for "hearing voices"

Clairfragrance

- Clear scent or clear smell
- Throat chakra
- Physical sense of smell/taste
- Archangel Jophiel, Archangel Gabriel, and Archangel Michael

Clairfragrance means clear scent or clear smell and is connected to your throat chakra, and mouth, teeth, tongue, and jaw.

Clairfragrance is the ability to pick up scents with the psychic nose that may be undetectable to the physical sense of smell. Clairfragance was more recently added to the list of clairs because so many people remarked on receiving angel messages through their sense of smell. Clairfragrance can show up as smelling cigarette smoke, baking bread, cotton candy, flowers, or even grandma's perfume when the physical source of the smell is simply not present. The angels use your sense of smell to guide your pain relief journey and support synchronicity.

When your clairfragrance channel is activated, it is teaching you to enter the present moment and pay close attention to the divine guidance you are receiving through all of your clair channels. Sometimes there is a message in the smell itself, and other times it is a sign to pause and check in with your angels' guidance. Your clairfragrance channel is reminding you of the sacred pause. When you receive a message through smell/taste, it is important to slow down and take note of other messages in your mind's eye, your body, or your inner dialogue.

Remember, this is where your angels are, right here and right now. Your angels are always guiding you to be more aware, present, and attuned, and they will use different smells to remind you of their presence. Like the old saying, "The nose knows," your angels can give you a quick message either through the scent itself or through the reminder to slow down and breathe deep.

The angels remind you that your olfactory senses are a discerning tool as you move toward smells that please you and are repelled by displeasing smells.

The shadow of clairfragrance is:

- Shame or unworthiness
- Embarrassment
- Disgrace or humiliation

- Judging yourself for your sensitivity
- Impatience

Clairsentience

- Clear feeling
- Sacral, navel, and solar plexus chakras
- Physical sense of touch
- Archangel Raziel, Archangel Haniel, and Archangel Raguel

Clairsentience is the ability to clearly feel energy such as emotions, thoughts, and of course, angels. Your clairsentience is directly connected with your abdominal organs, gut feelings, and receiving physical body sensations. This is the most common intuitive channel, yet it is often the most misunderstood. If you have experienced trauma or emotional abuse, as many earth angels have, this channel can be "muddy."

The angels remind you to recognize the difference between true angel guidance into your physical body (which offers comfort, support, or a warning) versus an emotional storm from an ego part. Angel messages will bring a certain level of comfort, calm, or relief, whereas a "gut feeling" that causes anxiety is a part of you trying to get your attention. Your angels will never share a message or guidance that evokes fear.

A knot in your stomach could mean, "Slow down, don't eat that," or, "Stay away from that person," but if it's an angel message, it won't terrify you. There is the wisdom of your body that knows what it needs to find balance. Then there are the parts that live in your body that need your angels' love. Clairsentient messages will be followed with a moment of peace, calm, or clarity within your body and will never increase anxiety or anger.

If the gut feeling is a warning of danger, the sensation will not bring fear or create panic. The best thing to do if you are not sure if a message is from the angels or your parts is to simply ask for more clarity. You can also ask for more signs and for more messages through your other clair channels to validate the guidance.

Clairsentient angel messages include:

- Angel bumps
- Shivers or chills
- Body temperature changes, like getting momentarily hot or chilled
- A strong or subtle pulling or tugging sensation in your stomach or heart
- Feeling light pressure on different body parts or chakras

Clairsentience can also mean feeling other people's emotions. If this channel is very open, you may feel others' emotions intensely, and sometimes it may feel like they are your own. As a sensitive soul, it's important to practice discernment within this intuitive channel and to not take on, absorb, or process anyone else's emotions.

Clairsentience gives you the gift of feeling your emotions deeply as an inner guide to the truth of the issue or situation. Receiving clairsentient messages is the most grounded of all the clairs because this channel is intimately connected with your physical body and lower body chakras. Your clairsentience can provide instant feedback from your environment. The clairsentience channel is the intuitive channel that lets you know you have received an angel message. When you get a clairvoyant, claircognizant, or clairaudient angel message, you always check to see how that message *feels* in your body. Your clairsentience creates a strong and important link between all five channels that provide angelic pain relief.

The shadow side of clairsentience is:

- Absorbing others' pain and strong emotions
- Feeling that you need to process others' emotions
- Feeling overwhelmed by other people's pain and anxiety
- Confusing the emotional pain of your parts in your body with angelic guidance
- Stress, tension, powerlessness, trauma, PTSD, or abuse

Now that you have learned all the direct ways your angels communicate with you, let's explore the indirect signs and messages your angels use to share with you on your pain relief journey.

Chapter Thirty

Indirect Angel Guidance

Indirect angel guidance consists of messages and support from your angels that comes from the external world. The purpose of indirect angel guidance is to validate your direct angel guidance and to provide guideposts along your path of pain relief. Remember, trauma and PTSD can block the flow of your intuition and keep the pain stuck in your body. Indirect angel guidance includes all the signs that remind you that you are on the right path. These outside validations increase your ability to trust your direct intuitive guidance. Just some examples of indirect angel guidance include:

- Signs
- Numbers
- Animals and birds
- Sacred objects
- Clouds and rainbows
- Music
- Other people
- Oracle cards

Signs

A sign is defined as an object, quality, or event whose presence or occurrence indicates the probable presence or occurrence of something else. Angel signs are everywhere, reminding you of their presence, love, and support. Your angels absolutely want you to know they are with you and that you are not alone. The signs you receive from your angels are a validation that you are on the right path of pain relief. There is nothing more reassuring than knowing you are exactly where you are supposed to be.

Signs from your angels are an indirect way for them to give you a message. Signs validate that your prayers are being answered. Signs can also be a gentle reminder to pray and ask for help. Each sign has a message, a meaning, and a purpose. Some common signs the angels use to confirm your intuition and ease your pain are repeating number sequences, animals, birds, coins, feathers, clouds, rainbows, songs, other people, and oracle cards.

Numbers

Numbers are a universal language. When you see the same number pattern repeating, like 22, 33, 44, or 444, 333, 11:11, or even 1234, the message is twofold. First, your angels are saying, "Come into the present moment," which is where your angels are. The present moment allows you to receive angelic pain relief. Second, your angels know the power of numbers and that there is a specific message within the number sequence itself. If you wish to explore these specific messages further, there are lots of books and websites about the meaning of each number and number sequencing.

Whether you see the numbers on a license plate (huge for me), a clock, a receipt, or a document, your angels are saying, "We are here; pay attention and receive our love now!"

Animals and Birds

Nature is a great healer. Your angels love when you go outside into the natural world because the stillness of a natural setting makes it easier to hear the whispers of the angels. The natural world provides so many signs to open your heart and mind to your angels' love. Seeing birds and animals while outside is always a validation of divine order and that you are watched over and protected. It's important to pay attention to what the animal or bird is doing as part of the healing message. If you would like to learn more, there are many books about animal medicine and messages.

Sacred Objects

Finding coins, feathers, heart shaped leaves, and other meaningful objects are all signs that your angels are near and encouraging you to move forward. Trusting that you are exactly where you are meant to be can soften your pain and create space for your angels' love to flow. Finding sacred objects, like "pennies from heaven," can let you know your prayer has been heard and answered. Receiving this confirmation calms your heart and mind, softens your pain, and allows you to receive more love from your angels.

Clouds and Rainbows

When you look up and see a rainbow or catch a cloud shaped like an angel or an animal, it's a huge validation of your angels' loving and eternal presence. It's comforting to know that no matter what pain or worry you are experiencing, there is an angel to help you with that. Rainbows are a universal message of hope and inspiration that can open your heart, allowing instant pain relief, if only for a moment. Acknowledging the signs with gratitude that your prayer is heard and answered invites more signs.

Music

Music is a powerful healer and another universal language. Your angels will often use music and songs to share messages. Pay attention if you hear the same song three times in a row because there is a pain relief message for you. Your angels may also guide you to healing music that can open your heart, calm your mind, and, therefore, soothe your pain.

Other People

Your angels know that when you hear a message from another fellow human, it can be quite transformational. At certain times, your angels will speak through other people to share pain relief messages. Again, pay attention to when you hear the same guidance three or more times from different people, as your angels are speaking to you through them. I have a cool story about that:

> *After our basement flooded for the third time, my first reaction was to feel pretty upset. This time, however, I was determined to see things differently. As I carried out all the wet carpeting, padding, and destroyed items, I prayed for a miracle.*
>
> *I kept repeating that this is a miracle, and that something really good will come from this destruction. I chanted, prayed, and asked the angels to turn this flood damage into a miracle as we cleaned up the mess.*
>
> *A few weeks later, I was sharing about the flood damage with a neighbor and they mentioned FEMA. Then, within a day or two of that conversation, two more people said the same thing. I got a gut feeling that this was the angels getting my attention, so I looked into it. Although we didn't meet the FEMA requirements, we were redirected to the SBA. We qualified for a low-interest government loan to repair our entire basement and get a flood control system that would prevent the type of flooding we had. Talk about a miracle from paying attention to the signs. Thank you, angels!*

Although signs from your angels are important, on the path of the earth angel, it's essential to receive your angels' message directly through your intuition. Indirect guidance from the angels is not supposed to replace your own direct angelic communication; it is supposed to support and enhance your direct intuitive channels, allowing them to open further.

You can ask for as many signs and synchronicities as you need to validate that you are on the right path. The more you notice angel signs, the more they will increase and guide you forward and away from pain toward the peace of your unstruck soul. In Sanskrit, the heart chakra translates to "anahata," which means unstruck. The "unstruck soul" means it is not hurt, not hit, and not struck or wounded.

Be mindful if you are asking for more signs from a place of fear or lack because you don't trust the Divine. Instead, pray to increase your ability to trust and receive your direct angel guidance and all the pain relieving angel signs.

Oracle Cards

Oracle cards are a form of indirect angel guidance that, in turn, opens your direct intuitive channels. Angel oracle cards provide focus, support, and validation of your own intuition. Working with angel oracle cards will empower your ability to receive healing and pain relief from your angels.

Angel oracle cards are meant to validate your intuition, not replace it. As an earth angel, direct angel guidance is the goal. You want to open and balance all five intuitive channels so you can receive divine downloads for a pain-free life.

However, the angels know that when you are in pain, your intuition can feel blocked or stuck. That is where oracle cards can come in. Oracle cards support the direct intuitive guidance you are receiving and validate your inner knowing. Angel oracle cards are discussed at length in chapter thirteen.

Chapter Thirty-one

Take Action on the Angel Guidance You Receive

Receiving your angels' messages will require you to take action on the guidance, whether direct or indirect. Sometimes the actions are very small, and you may not even realize they are angel steps. For example, your angels may guide you to eat or walk slower to reduce pain. Your angels may guide you to take a 15-minute nature walk in the middle of the day so you can hear them more clearly. Your angels may suggest you pause and re-devote before you talk to a challenging loved one or co-worker so you feel more loving and centered when you speak.

When you are first learning to listen to angelic whispers to heal pain, some of the steps may seem illogical or not directly related to the pain relief you seek. It is common to ignore or dismiss the guidance as you strengthen your intuitive channels of receiving. Remember, sometimes the action required is non-action. Your angelic pain relief guidance may be to take a nap, go to sleep earlier, or be in silence. Your angels are devoted to healing your pain and will consistently offer their pain relief messages.

Once you begin to recognize the way in which your angels communicate with you, it takes faith to follow through on the divinely-guided steps. Your angels know it takes trust, faith, and courage to make changes and to heal pain naturally. That's why the angels suggest small, doable action steps. The small, sometimes illogical, but always loving and practical angel steps are designed to build your faith in their guidance. Eventually, when you are guided to take a leap of faith, you have already laid the foundation.

Your angels' pain-relieving messages can become diminished if you do not take the appropriate action steps they are guiding you to take. You will rarely receive the next step until you take the one already given. No worries, your angels will lovingly repeat themselves until you take the divinely-guided action step. Your angels are infinitely patient with your human journey.

Your angels know exactly what you need to heal. They also know it takes a brave heart to listen when your parts are in pain and want to dismiss or ignore the guidance. Receiving from your angels to heal pain in your body is not for the faint of heart.

It takes courage to trust and receive divine guidance from your angels. You need a brave heart to take the big and small action steps. Of course, you always have the free will to choose to not take the step. Your angels will never judge your choices. They will wait patiently until you summon the courage and faith to lean into the divine love they are sending. It's comforting to know that your angels are with you, lighting your path of healing each step of the way.

Chapter Thirty-two

Steps for Practice Four: Receive and Trust Your Intuition

There are six steps for Practice Four: Receive and Trust Your Intuition. Although steps two through six can build on each other, they can also be used independently to hone one of your intuitive channels. The steps for this practice include:

Step 1: Intention and Invitation

Step 2: Receive and Trust Your Claircognizance

Step 3: Receive and Trust Your Clairvoyance

Step 4: Receive and Trust Your Clairaudience

Step 5: Receive and Trust Your Clairfragrance

Step 6: Receive and Trust Your Clairsentience

Step 1: Choose Your Intention and Invite the Archangels of Receive and Trust Your Intuition

Remember, energy follows intention. Choose how you want to feel so the angels of your intention surround you. Your intention, or fuel, becomes the anchor for you to receive angelic pain relief. In this step, you will:

- Choose your intention
- Recite Archangel Invitation
- Pause, breathe, and receive
- Express gratitude

The Archangel Invitation I created is designed to welcome the medicine of the archangels of Receive and Trust Your Intuition: Archangel Uriel, Archangel Raziel, Archangel Orion, and Archangel Jophiel. Each of these archangels carries a specific medicine, as follows:

Archangel Uriel—Angel of Hope

- Illumination and innocence
- Divine thought
- Claircognizance

Archangel Raziel—Angel of Alchemy

- Magic, revealing, and personal power
- Spiritual understanding of pain
- Clairvoyance and clairsentience

Archangel Orion—Angel of Miracles

- Miracles and manifestation
- Clears negativity with unconditional love
- Clairaudience

Archangel Jophiel—Angel of Beauty

- Beautify your thoughts
- Connects you to the heartbeat of Mother Earth
- Clarity, aura clearing, and clairfragrance

In order for the archangels to enter your aura and offer pain relief, you need to ask for and invite their help. You can use any number of prayers to invite the archangels' loving support. The invitation below is designed to welcome the medicine of the archangels of Receive and Trust Your Intuition. Feel free to change or modify the invitation.

I invite the help and healing transmissions of Archangel Uriel, Archangel Raziel, Archangel Orion, and Archangel Jophiel to guide and protect me. Thank you for blessing and opening my five intuitive channels so I can trust and receive my intuition. I welcome your loving guidance into all five clair channels now so I can take the next pain-relieving step forward. I ask that the healing I receive today be shared with all my relations in all directions of time.

After you recite the invitation, take three deep breaths. Pause and let yourself receive the archangels' loving presence into your body and any points of pain. It's common when you are first inviting the archangels into your space to feel uncertainty, self-doubt, or skepticism about receiving pain relief from the angels. Be gentle and patient with the process. Humans say practice makes perfect; the angels say practice makes better.

Step 2: Receive and Trust Your Claircognizance

As an earth angel, you are supported in working with your direct angel guidance, starting with claircognizance. In this step, you will:

- Invite Archangel Uriel's medicine
- Receive through crown chakra
- Trust your claircognizance
- Take action

We begin by inviting Archangel Uriel:

Thank you, Archangel Uriel, for bringing me the medicine of hope, illumination, and innocence. I invite the brilliant golden light of Archangel Uriel to enlighten and flow into my crown, brain, and nervous system so I can receive and trust my claircognizance. I allow the angels of hope, innocence, and illumination to infuse my aura and my crown chakra with their loving light. I am ready, willing, and able to receive, trust, and take action on my claircognizant thoughts.

You can receive through your crown chakra simply with your intention to do so. Set your intention to receive angelic innocence into your crown. Visualize your crown like a lotus flower and see or feel each petal opening to the light of the angels. Invite your crown chakra to receive the light of Archangel Uriel, which awakens your claircognizance to brilliant ideas and divine thought. Inhale illumination and hope into your crown, and exhale negativity and despair.

You can also imagine your crown chakra as a healing temple that you can enter at will. Your crown chakra temple, like all chakra temples, is a healing and alchemical space which contains sacred energy, wisdom, and light. Welcome Archangel Uriel and your guardian angels to bless and empower your crown chakra temple, helping you release the suppressed energy of guilt, negativity, and illusions that cause pain.

You can also receive through your crown chakra by accessing mental relaxation. Slowing down your mind by focusing on your breath will help you discern angelic thoughts from egoic thoughts. Consciously choosing angel thoughts will further open your crown chakra, aligning your mind with Divine mind.

Trusting your claircognizance begins with being aware of your thoughts and ideas. You can trust the thoughts of love, peace, and hope that encourage pain relief. You can amplify your claircognizance by consciously releasing thoughts that make you feel guilty, negative, hopeless, or despair to Archangel Uriel.

You can build self-trust by affirming that you trust your intuitive channel of claircognizance. Affirm often, "I fully trust my claircognizance. I trust all pain-relieving angel thoughts."

Taking action requires courage and will strengthen this intuitive channel.

Taking action on your claircognizance looks like:

- Listening to the angel thoughts
- Consciously releasing negative or non-serving thoughts

- Taking steps forward based on the angel thoughts
- Thanking Archangel Uriel

Step 3: Receive and Trust Your Clairvoyance

As an earth angel, you are supported in working with your direct angel guidance as you move on to clairvoyance. In this step, you will:

- Invite Archangel Raziel's medicine
- Receive through third eye
- Trust your clairvoyance
- Take action

We start by inviting Archangel Raziel:

Thank you, Archangel Raziel, for bringing me the medicine of unconditional trust and alchemy. I invite the rainbow ray of Archangel Raziel to bless and heal my physical eyes, master glands, and third eye so I can receive and trust my clairvoyance. I allow the angels of unconditional trust and alchemy to infuse my aura and third eye with their healing light so I can receive, trust, and take action on my clairvoyant visions.

Set your intention to receive angelic trust through your third eye chakra. Breathe and receive the rainbow ray into your third eye to release worry, distrust, and self-doubt that may block your inner vision. Inhale trust into your third eye and exhale worry and doubt out of your third eye chakra.

Visualize your third eye as a sacred temple that you can enter anytime. There are healing chambers within the temple where your pain parts can rest and receive healing. Visualize Archangel Raziel clearing and empowering your inner vision as past pain and wounds are released. You can open and receive through your third eye by visualizing it as a physical eye opening to the light.

You can also receive through your third eye by accessing mental relaxation. Inhale for a count of four, suspend the breath for one count, exhale for a count of four, and then suspend the breath for one count at the bottom of your exhale. The space between your breath calms your mind and opens your inner vision.

Trusting your clairvoyance happens when you receive the inner vision, mental movie, and images in your mind's eye. You can trust the images of your inner world that lead to pain relief. You can amplify your clairvoyance by consciously releasing worry, distrust, self-doubt, and worst case scenarios from your inner vision to Archangel Raziel. Imagine handing your worries to Archangel Raziel, who carries them to the heart of Source for transformation.

You can build self-trust by affirming that you trust your intuitive channel of clairvoyance. Affirm often, "I fully trust my clairvoyance. I trust my inner vision to lead to angelic pain relief."

Taking action on your clairvoyance can look like:

- Honoring your inner vision
- Being willing to see your pain parts
- Taking steps forward on your inner vision
- Thanking Archangel Raziel

Step 4: Receive and Trust Your Clairaudience

As an earth angel, you are supported in working with your direct angel guidance as you move on to clairaudience. In this step, you will:

- Invite Archangel Orion's medicine
- Receive through ear chakras
- Trust your clairaudience
- Take action

We start with inviting Archangel Orion:

Thank you, Archangel Orion, for bringing me the medicine of miracles and manifestation. I invite the midnight blue light of Archangel Orion to flow into my physical ears and inner ear organs so I can receive and trust my clairaudience. I allow the angels of miracles, manifestation, and unconditional love to infuse my aura and ear chakras with their healing light so I can receive, trust, and take action on the clairaudient messages and reveal the miracles.

Set your intention to receive angelic love and compassion into your ear chakras. Breathe and receive Archangel Orion's loving light into your physical ears and ear chakras to release the old programs, judgments, or anything painful you have ever heard, thought, or felt.

Imagine your ear chakras as a temple you can enter to receive clear, audible angel messages. Within the ear chakra temple, you may observe shadowy places where past negative thinking, self-judgments, or criticism is stored. You are safe to see this painful pattern and the parts connected with it. Visualize Archangel Orion, Archangel Zadkiel, and Archangel Michael radiating compassion and love to these pain parts clearing your space.

You can receive through your ear chakras by accessing spiritual relaxation. Spiritual relaxation is surrender. It supports you in surrendering and releasing defensiveness, struggle, and harmful thoughts so that you can trust the benevolent divine plan unfolding. Spiritual relaxation invites space for grace and miracles to manifest.

Trusting your clairaudience happens when you receive the audible messages from your angels that are answers to your pain relief prayers. Angel thoughts will create a feeling of peace, calm, and ease. Anything else is wounded parts or old programs. You can amplify your clairaudience channel by consciously releasing past negative thinking and painful or hurtful thoughts, memories, or inner dialogue to Archangel Orion.

You can build self-trust by affirming that you trust your intuitive channel of clairaudience. Affirm often, "I fully trust my clairaudience. I trust my inner voice to lead to angelic pain relief."

Taking action on your clairaudience can look like:

- Being willing to hear the voice of your angels, your body, and your parts
- Taking the step the audible message guides you to take
- Using mantra, meditation, and music to elevate this channel
- Thanking Archangel Orion

Step 5: Receive and Trust Your Clairfragrance

As an earth angel, you are supported in working with your direct angel guidance as you move on to clairfragrance. In this step, you will:

- Invite Archangel Jophiel's medicine
- Receive through throat chakra
- Trust your clairfragrance
- Take action

We begin with inviting Archangel Jophiel:

Thank you, Archangel Jophiel, for bringing me the medicine of clarity, patience, and worthiness. I invite the magenta light of Archangel Jophiel to flow into my nose, mouth, throat, and lungs, bringing clarity, calm, and restoring my inner beauty so I can receive and trust my clairfragrance. I allow the angels of clarity, patience, and worthiness to infuse my aura and throat chakra with their healing light so I can receive, trust, and take action on my clairfragrant messages.

Set your intention to receive angelic patience, worthiness, and clarity into your throat chakra. Breathe and receive the magenta light of Archangel Jophiel into your nose, mouth, jaw, throat, and lungs. Inhale divine worth and patience and, exhale shame, disgrace, and unworthiness.

Visualize your throat chakra like a beautiful flower opening its petals to the light and revealing your inner beauty and divine worth. You can also imagine your throat chakra as a temple to enter in which you can be refreshed. You may smell the sweet scent of blooming flowers or even taste the sweetness of the fresh air. It is okay if you do not smell or taste anything right away. Welcome Archangel Jophiel to help you release the suppressed energies of shame, unworthiness, disgrace, or impatience so you can realize your divine worth.

You can receive through your throat chakra by accessing physical relaxation. When you relax your muscles from your bones, you enter the present moment. In this present moment, you can open your senses and tune in to your clairfragrance channel.

Trusting your clairfragrance happens when you notice smells and tastes with curiosity. It is important on the path of the earth angel to not dismiss this subtle channel. A clairfragrant message may precede an intuitive message that comes from another clair channel. The smell/taste is a sign for you to slow down and come into the present moment. Clairfragrance is a gentle nudge to pay attention and trust the next pain relief message.

You can build self-trust by affirming that you trust your intuitive channel of clairfragrance. Affirm often, "I fully trust my clairfragrance. I trust my sacred sense of smell and taste to lead to angelic pain relief."

Taking action on your clairfragrance looks like:

- Observing what you smell and taste during and after prayer

- Allowing the smell to guide your next steps
- Acknowledging when you have received a clairfragrance message
- Thanking Archangel Jophiel

Step 6: Receive and Trust Your Clairsentience

As an earth angel, you are supported in working with your direct angel guidance as you finish up with clairsentience. In this step, you will:

- Invite Archangel Raziel's medicine
- Receive through sacral, navel, and solar plexus chakras
- Trust your clairsentience
- Take action

We begin with inviting Archangel Raziel:

> *Thank you, Archangel Raziel, for bringing me the medicine of revealing, peace, and personal power. I invite the rainbow ray of Archangel Raziel to flow into my internal organs, revealing my inner peace and power. I allow the angels of revelation, peace, and power to infuse my aura and lower chakras with their healing light. I am ready, willing, and able to receive, trust, and take action on my clairsentient feelings.*

Set your intention to receive angelic ease into your reproductive organs, sacrum, lower spine, and sacral chakra. Breathe and receive the rainbow ray into your sacral chakra, releasing abuse and powerlessness. Inhale ease and exhale powerlessness.

Set your intention to receive angelic ease into your stomach, adrenals, kidneys, bladder, and navel chakra. Breathe and receive the rainbow ray into your navel chakra, releasing stress, tension, PTSD, and trauma. Inhale ease and exhale stress.

Set your intention to receive angelic peace and forgiveness into your liver, gallbladder, pancreas, stomach, spleen, adrenals, and solar plexus chakra. Breathe and receive the rainbow ray into your solar plexus chakra, releasing anger, judgment, resentment, and harshness. Inhale forgiveness and exhale anger.

Visualize your sacral, navel, and solar plexus chakras as beautiful temples you can engage with to experience the physical effects and sensations of your angels. Welcome Archangel Raziel and Archangel Raguel to help you release suppressed emotions, such as anger, stress, or trauma that are causing you pain and diminishing your clairsentience.

You can receive through your lower chakras and belly by accessing emotional relaxation. Emotional relaxation makes space for all of your emotions to flow and be expressed with grace. When your emotions calm, your body relaxes. When your body relaxes, you can safely feel the pain and allow it to release.

Trusting your clairsentience happens when you honor your emotions and feelings. This doesn't mean you drown or wallow in those feelings. Trusting clairsentience takes spiritual maturity and discernment. Honoring your true feelings makes room for more joy, and joy transforms pain. You can amplify your clairsentience channel by releasing stress, trauma, anger, or judgment from your gut to Archangel Raziel and Archangel Raguel. The angels remind you to be patient with the releasing process, as anger is the most difficult emotion for the human body to release once suppressed.

You can build self-trust by affirming that you trust your intuitive channel of clairsentience. Affirm often, "I fully trust my clairsentience. I trust my gut feelings and emotions to lead to angelic pain relief."

Taking action on your clairsentience can look like:

- Creating space to feel and emote
- Not absorbing or processing others' emotions
- Being completely honest with yourself about how you feel
- Tending to your emotional needs
- Thanking Archangel Raziel and Archangel Raguel

Congratulations on completing the steps to receiving angelic pain relief. You are an amazing angel receiver and your angels are celebrating your devotion to healing your pain with angel love. Keep shining your tender, loving heart light, earth angel. You are seen and you are so very loved.

Chapter Thirty-three

Receive and Trust Your Intuition: Guided Angel Meditation

Each practice has its own guided angel meditation to support and reinforce the practice itself as well as your connection to your angels. By using these guided angel meditations, you open yourself to receiving more of your angels' love to heal your pain.

Begin with your breath. Inhale deeply and exhale completely, relaxing your shoulders as you exhale. Thank your body for serving you so well and feel your soul inside your body. As you breathe, feel the vastness and love of your soul expand outside of your body, into your aura, and up toward your angels. Feel your angels welcoming all of your parts.

Invite all your angels, guardian angels, allies, beloved ancestors, and the archangels of Receive and Trust Your Intuition: Archangel Uriel, the angel of claircognizance; Archangel Jophiel, the angel of clairfragrance; Archangel Raziel, the angel of clairvoyance and clairsentience; and Archangel Orion, the angel of clairaudience. Invite the light of God, Source, Creator, Creatrix, and all the healing angels to be here now. Say, "Thank you for guiding and protecting me with your healing light for my highest good and highest healing. I am the keeper of my mind and body, and I welcome only those angels who love me unconditionally."

Renew your devotion. Gently place your hands over your heart, the gateway to your angels' love. Say silently, "I am devoted to receiving intuitive downloads from my angels." Open your heart to your angels' love. Align your mind with Divine mind. Receive your angels' devotion for you.

Relax and cherish your body. Give yourself permission to relax as you trust that you are exactly where you are meant to be. As you breathe, welcome physical relaxation as you soften your muscles from your bones and release tension for your neck, back, and shoulders.

Visualize roots of light flowing through your legs, out of the soles of your feet, and deep into the heart of the earth. Feel mother earth receiving you. Trust the wisdom of your roots to connect with the perfect crystals, tree roots, and ancestor medicine for you today, amplifying your ability to release more and receive more.

As you breathe, welcome emotional relaxation as your guardian angels make room for all of your feelings, emotions, and parts. As your emotions calm, your body relaxes even more.

As you breathe, welcome mental relaxation as you slow down your thoughts. Gently focus on your breath. Follow the length of your breath to the top of your inhalation and follow the length of your breath to the bottom of your exhalation deep in your belly. Notice the space between your thoughts where all creativity, divine solutions, your intuition, and miracles reside. Open and balance each chakra with the medicine of trust.

As you breathe, welcome spiritual relaxation as you surrender into the arms of your angels and expand your auric field. Trust the benevolent divine plan unfolding for your highest good and for all those you love.

Release and lead with your heart. In this deep state of relaxation, allow any physical, emotional, mental, and spiritual pain, distrust, or worry to release from your body through your breath, down through your roots, and gently out of your muscles, bones, and cells through your chakras and aura toward the alchemy of your angels' love.

Trust that releasing happens in layers, and it's totally normal for your body to twitch or shudder and for your emotions to rise and fall as you release. Allow your angels to bring your heart and mind into unison. You are safe to release, release, release.

Receive and trust your intuition. As you breathe, invite Archangel Uriel to bless, open, and align your crown chakra. You are safe to release guilt and negativity and receive innocence and joy, empowering your claircognizance. Your thoughts are clearly connected to your angels. Affirm, "I am aligned with Divine mind."

As you breathe, invite Archangel Raziel to bless, open, and align your third eye chakra. You are safe to release worry and self-doubt and receive unconditional trust, empowering your clairvoyance. Your mind's eye can clearly see divine love. Affirm, "I trust my inner vision to see the love within and around me."

As you breathe, invite Archangel Orion to bless, open, and align your ear chakras. You are safe to release pain and hurt and receive positivity, empowering your clairaudience. Your ears are attuned to the highest angelic frequencies. Affirm, "I manifest miracles by clearly hearing the voice of my angels."

As you breathe, invite Archangel Jophiel to bless, open, and align your throat chakra. You are safe to release shame and impatience and receive divine worthiness, empowering your clairfragrance. Your sense of smell/taste is attuned to your angels' love. Affirm, "I trust my sacred sense of smell to lead the way to my highest good."

As you breathe, invite Archangel Raziel to bless, open, and align sacral, navel, and solar plexus chakras. You are safe to release stress, trauma, anger, and pain and receive ease and forgiveness, empowering your clairsentience. Your physical and emotional feelings are connected to your angels. Affirm, "I trust my gut feelings as accurate angel guidance."

You are safe and spiritually protected to trust what you see, feel, hear, know, sense, and smell in the sacred moment in time. Trust all the ways in which your angels are communicating with you. You are safe to be tender, vulnerable, and open to your angels' love. You are safe to receive, receive, receive.

Receive a final blessing of deep compassion, unconditional trust, and healing from the archangels of Receive and Trust Your Intuition and your own guardian angels. Say, "I ask that all the healing I receive today be shared with all my relations in all directions of time."

Take a cleansing breath, in and out. Gently bow to your angels as you bring your hands to prayer mudra (position) and feel them bow to you with love, devotion, and deep compassion, sealing your meditation with a Namaste (or an Amen, or other word you prefer).

Conclusion

My personal intention for writing this book was to help you heal your pain naturally, whether that pain was physical or emotional, with the love of your angels. I am an Angel Ambassador, here to bring the love of the Divine onto the earth in a grounded and tangible way by healing your body, the home of your soul.

Through writing this book and sharing my story, I've experienced the power of the angels to transform pain into peace and joy. Sharing my challenges and initiations has allowed me to transform my wounds into wisdom. I channeled the wisdom gained from my difficulties into the creation of each practice in this book so you can be healed by unconditional angelic love. Each personal story taught me how to access angel love to heal my body.

My hope is that this book has shared the importance and benefits of learning how to receive love and healing from your angels. Accepting your angels' love and pain-relieving messages into your body and heart allows you to heal physical or emotional pain. This book was designed to help you create a self-care practice that honors your whole self while sharing compassion with others to transmute pain into joy.

This book was created to support you, the courageous earth angel who is ready to reclaim your magnificence, shine your light, and heal your body naturally with angelic pain relief. I want to thank each and every one of you who has invested your time, energy, and whole heart into reading my first book.

I hope that you have learned the importance of the role your angels play in healing your pain. Your unwavering faith in your angels' love for you allows them to act as miracle workers in your life. Your angels encourage you to trust that as you focus on your own personal healing, you are healing the world. I invite you to relax, release, and receive love from your angels every day to heal your precious body and awaken your heart's miraculous medicine. Always remember: You are loved beyond measure.

Resources

The Archangels of Each Practice

Practice One: Renew Your Devotion

- ❖ Archangel Michael's Medicine—"He who is like God"—Archangel Michael offers flawless protection to help you reclaim your magnificence and helps with cutting the cords of fear and pain with the sword of truth.
- ❖ Archangel Metatron's Medicine—"The One Who Serves behind God's Throne"—Metatron's cube (a glowing ball of healing light and sacred geometric shapes) supports chakra clearing, supports sensitive children, and aids with organization, prioritizing, and building.
- ❖ Archangel Ariel's Medicine—"Lioness of God"—Archangel Ariel, the angel of compassion who helps with courage and healing on all levels. Archangel Ariel awakens the soul's mission to help you achieve prosperity and abundance.
- ❖ Archangel Sandalphon's Medicine—"Brother Together"—Archangel Sandalphon, the angel of gentleness who brings gratitude and devotion. Archangel Sandalphon anchors

your soul into your body, grounds your body to the earth through your earth star chakra, and carries your prayers to the Divine.

Practice Two: Relax and Cherish Your Body

- Archangel Gabriel's Medicine—"God Is My Strength"—Archangel Gabriel, who presents as both masculine and feminine, helps with clear communication, both verbal and nonverbal. Gabriel is the archangel of creativity, supporting self-expression through outlets like journaling, writing, and singing. Gabriel encourages physical relaxation and nurtures your inner child.
- Archangel Haniel's Medicine—"Glory of God"—Archangel Haniel, the angel of sensitivity, is an empath protector who helps with emotional relaxation, honoring your parts and emotions, and sealing aura leaks.
- Archangel Raphael's Medicine—"Who God Heals"—Archangel Raphael is the divine physician who supports mental relaxation, opening chakras, and a balanced and healthy lifestyle. Raphael creates miracles through divine intervention, inviting healing on all levels.
- Archangel Raguel's Medicine—"Friend of God"—Archangel Raguel, the angel of divine order, is the angel of relationship harmony who encourages spiritual relaxation, auric cleaning, and cooperation.

Practice Three: Release and Lead With Your Heart

- Archangel Chamuel's Medicine—"He Who Sees God"—Archangel Chamuel is the angel of peace and self-love who helps to release hurt, heartache, or grief so you can love with your whole self.

- Archangel Zadkiel's Medicine—"Righteousness of God"—Archangel Zadkiel, the angel of compassion, transformation, and clairaudience, is the spiritual professor angel who accesses ancient knowledge from your soul star chakra and the Akashic records. Zadkiel is one of the keepers of the Violet Flame of transformation.
- Archangel Azrael's Medicine—"Angel of Comfort"—Archangel Azrael, the angel of comfort and wisdom, is the ultimate grief counselor angel who assists souls in crossing over at the time of their physical death by releasing pain. Azrael helps you connect with loved ones on the other side.
- Archangel Jeremiel's Medicine—"Mercy of God"—Archangel Jeremiel is the angel of mercy and forgiveness who assists in overcoming difficulties and challenges, transforming bitterness and resentment into grace and mercy by opening your heart.

Practice Four: Receive and Trust Your Intuition

- Archangel Uriel's Medicine—"The Light of God"—Archangel Uriel is the angel of illumination, brilliant ideas, hope, and claircognizance who helps you shine your light even brighter. With Archangel Uriel's help, you can open your crown chakra and tap into innocence and divine wisdom.
- Archangel Raziel's Medicine—"Secrets of God"—Archangel Raziel, the angel of alchemy, clairvoyance, clairsentience, and magic, helps you take back your power as a supreme manifestor and assists your alchemical work by helping you turn your ideas into gold.

- ❖ Archangel Orion's Medicine—"Rising in the Sky"—Archangel Orion, the angel of miracles, manifestation, and clairaudience, helps you clear negativity so you can hear the wisdom of your angels. With Archangel Orion's protection, you can shift your perception from fear to love.
- ❖ Archangel Jophiel's Medicine—"Beauty of God"—Archangel Jophiel, the angel of beauty, patience, and clairfragrance, connects you with the heartbeat of Mother Earth, helping you slow down and savor the moment by beautifying your thoughts and clearing unworthiness.

13 Spiritual Chakras

1. Earth Star Chakra—Archangels: Sandalphon and Roquiel; Color(s): Black and White; Element(s): Earth—Your earth star chakra is an entry point for your energetic roots to connect to the earth and all its treasures. It's designed to ground your body to the earth and anchor your soul into your body.
2. Root or Base Chakra—Archangels: Michael, Faith, Gabriel, Hope, and Ariel; Color(s): Platinum (5D) and Red (3D); Element(s): Earth—Your root chakra is the home to your energetic roots designed to provide a foundation that allows you to feel safe and secure in your body as well as grounded to the earth.
3. Sacral Chakra—Archangels: Gabriel and Hope; Color(s): Tender Pink (5D) and Orange (3D); Element(s): Water—

Your sacral chakra is designed to empower and support your creativity and clairsentience.

4. Navel Chakra—Archangels: Gabriel and Hope; Color(s): Bright Orange (5D) and Orange (3D); Element(s): Water—Your navel chakra is designed to ignite your passion for life, bring ease and flow, and encourage balance and harmony.
5. Solar Plexus Chakra—Archangels: Uriel, Aurora, Raziel, and Jochara; Color(s): Deep Gold With Rainbow Lights (5D) and Yellow (3D); Element(s): Fire—Your solar plexus chakra is designed to be the home of your personal power, support angelic action steps, and house the fire in your body.
6. Heart Chakra—Archangels: Chamuel, Charity, and Ariel; Color(s): White (5D), Green (3D), and Pink (3D); Element(s): Water and Wind—Your heart chakra has an infinite capacity to create sacred space, and it is designed to be an alchemical space of unconditional love.
7. Throat Chakra—Archangels: Michael, Faith, Gabriel, and Hope; Colors: Royal Blue (5D) and Light Blue (3D); Element(s): Wind and Water—Your throat chakra is designed to be the center of communication and creative expression, allowing you to speak your personal truth with love and self-worth.
8. Third Eye Chakra—Archangels: Raphael, Mother Mary, Raziel, and Jochara; Color(s): Crystal-Clear (5D) and Royal Blue (3D); Element(s): Wind—Your third eye chakra is designed to create a mental movie or image of each chakra temple and receive clear images from your angels.
9. Ear Chakras—Archangels: Zadkiel, Amethyst, Michael, and Faith; Color(s): Violet (5D); Element(s): Storm—The ear

chakras are the home of the intuitive channel clairaudience and are designed to hear and receive the whispers of your body and to help you clearly hear the voice of your angels.

10. Crown Chakra—Archangels: Jophiel, Christine, Uriel, and Aurora; Color(s): Crystal-Clear (5D) and Purple/Violet (3D); Element(s): Storm—Your crown chakra is designed to be the home of your intuitive channel, claircognizance, and support your direct access to divine thought.
11. Causal Chakra—Archangels: Christel and Mallory; Color(s): White (5D); Element(s): Storm—The causal chakra is the halo chakra and is designed to support your crown in staying open to the high vibration of the angels and allow the high frequencies of divine love to stimulate your crown, brain, and nerves.
12. Soul Star Chakra—Archangels: Zadkiel, Amethyst, Lavender, Mariel, and Ariel; Color(s): Magenta (5D); Element(s): Storm—Your soul star chakra is designed to carry the blueprint of your soul's mission; it contains your karma (patterns) and your dharma (greater purpose).
13. Stellar Gateway Chakra—Archangels: Metatron and Seraphina; Color(s): Deepest Gold into Orange (5D); Element(s): Storm—Your stellar gateway chakra is designed to receive direct messages from God, store your prayers, and receive your answered prayers.

Cord Cutting for Angelic Pain Relief

Step 1: Devote and lead with your heart

- Hands over heart, say, "*I am devoted to receiving love from my angels.*"
- Welcome your angelic team to surround you, including Archangel Michael.
- Make a heart connection with the person you are corded to.
- Ask the question: *What is the cord that is depleting me the most?* Be very gentle and self-loving. No judgment.

Step 2: Relax and accept

- Surrender to non-resistance by relaxing your body and mind.
- Accept the pain, the cord, other person, situation, or memory. It may sound counterintuitive as you want to cut and release the cord, but whatever you resist persists.
- Welcome the angels of acceptance.
- Observe the cord before you cut it. Let yourself see the cord and acknowledge the cord's service. The cord will not hurt you. It may have been there for years or even lifetimes. Observe as many details about the cord with curiosity. Notice if the cord has:
  - Color
  - Texture
  - Temperature
  - Thickness
  - Movement
- What does the cord look like? Some examples include: tree roots, tubing, chains, ropes, threads
- What part of your body or chakra do you feel, sense, or see?

Step 3: Receive the blessing

- Recognize the gifts, blessings, and lessons from the cord.
- See the higher truth of the cord.
- Ask questions to receive the blessing. (Don't rush this step. Take your time.)
  - What is the lesson of this cord?
  - What is the blessing from this cord?
  - What is the gift from this cord?
  - What lesson am I learning from this cord?
  - How is this cord a miracle in my life ?

Step 4: Release and cut the cords

- Declare, command, affirm, or state, *"It is now done!"*
- Visualize Archangel Michael with the sword of light cutting the cords between you and the person, situation, or memory.
- Affirm it is done again, and thank the other person.
- Invite Archangel Raphael to fill the space where the cord was cut or dissolved with healing green light, like putting arnica ointment on a sore muscle.

A Note From Jill

Throughout my journey, I have loved returning to different quotes to remind me of what's true and what's important. Here are a few of my favorites. I hope you find them as helpful as I have.

– Namaste, Jill

(PS: You can tear this page out and carry it with you!)

"The wound is the place the light enters you."

– Rumi

"The pains you feel are messengers. Listen to them."

– Rumi

"The cure for the pain is in the pain."

– Rumi

"We cannot solve problems by using the same kind of thinking we used when we created them."

– Albert Einstein (in other words: "The mind that created the problem cannot solve the problem.")

"There are only two ways to live your life. One is as though nothing is a miracle. The other is as though everything is a miracle."

– Albert Einstein

Acknowledgments

There are so many to acknowledge in the creation and birth of this book.

I want to acknowledge my parts that have healed. Thank you for trusting my soul and my angels to share my story and my truth. I want to thank my awesome celestial team of angels and allies for helping me love more, cheering me on from the heavens every time.

I truly acknowledge my earth angel team, who, as I like to say, "put me back together again." Thank you for your support, love, and encouragement that helped me keep going when I wanted to quit, hide, or give up.

I want to acknowledge my earth angel clients and students who trusted my medicine. Thank you for your trust, love, courage, and vulnerability that helped bring my angel medicine and this book to life. I see you!

I want to acknowledge my whole publishing team, all my professional colleagues, and the healing centers that supported my angel work. Thank you for believing in me.

I want to acknowledge my family for their patience, positivity, and unconditional love and prayers that grounded me and allowed me to share my medicine. Thank you for trusting and loving me. Thank you for supporting my legacy of love.

I want to acknowledge my friends who saw my light when I couldn't. Thank you for your trust, love, compassion, and most of all, for letting me be me.

I deeply acknowledge my husband and soulmate, who told me when we first met, "It's faith or fear, not both." Thank you for loving all my parts, reconnecting me with God and my faith, and for always having compassion, patience, and unconditional love for me. I love you!

About the Author

Jill Kempner was in the healing field for almost 20 years before evolving into an Angel Professional. She began her career as a massage therapist and yoga teacher before starting her Reiki training, which was when she really began to embrace the energy medicine she practices today. In 2008, she was introduced to the angels which began her lifelong journey of working with them and becoming an Angel Professional. She organically merged her angel work with her Integrated Energy Therapy (IET) training, and her practice evolved naturally from there.

As an Angel Professional, Jill focuses on teaching and helping her clients "relax, release, and receive," to heal pain.

Jill happily lives in Illinois with her husband, two kids, and their two cats.